MTTC 17
Biology
Teacher Certification Exam

By: Sharon Wynne, M.S
Southern Connecticut State University

XAMonline, INC.
Boston

To obtain permission(s) to use the material from this work for any purpose including workshops or seminars, please submit a written request to:

XAMonline, Inc.
21 Orient Ave.
Melrose, MA 02176
Toll Free 1-800-509-4128
Email: info@xamonline.com
Web www.xamonline.com
Fax: 1-781-662-9268

Library of Congress Cataloging-in-Publication Data

Wynne, Sharon A.
    Biology 17: Teacher Certification / Sharon A. Wynne. -2nd ed.
    ISBN 978-1-58197-954-1
    1. Biology 17.   2. Study Guides.   3. MTTC
    4. Teachers' Certification & Licensure.   5. Careers

Disclaimer:
The material presented in this publication is the sole works of XAMonline and was created independently from the National Education Association, Educational Testing Service, or any State Department of Education, National Evaluation Systems or other testing affiliates.

Between the time of publication and printing, state specific standards, testing formats, and website information may change that is not included in part or in whole within this product. XAMonline developed the sample test questions and they reflect similar content as on real tests; however, they are not former tests. XAMonline assembles content that aligns with state standards but makes no claims nor guarantees regarding test performance. Numerical scores are determined by testing companies such as NES or ETS and then are compared with individual state standards. A passing score varies from state to state.

Printed in the United States of America

MTTC: Biology 17
ISBN: 978-1-58197-954-1

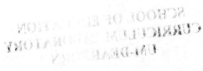

Table of Contents

Great Study and Testing Tips!

What to study in order to prepare for the subject assessments is the focus of this study guide but equally important is *how* you study.

You can increase your chances of truly mastering the information by taking some simple, but effective steps.

Study Tips:

1. Some foods aid the learning process. Foods such as milk, nuts, seeds, rice, and oats help your study efforts by releasing natural memory enhancers called CCKs (*cholecystokinins*) composed of *tryptophan*, *choline*, and *phenylalanine*. All of these chemicals enhance the neurotransmitters associated with memory. Before studying, try a light, protein-rich meal of eggs, turkey, and fish. All of these foods release the memory enhancing chemicals. The better the connections, the more you comprehend.

Likewise, before you take a test, stick to a light snack of energy boosting and relaxing foods. A glass of milk, a piece of fruit, or some peanuts all release various memory-boosting chemicals and help you to relax and to focus on the subject at hand.

2. Learn to take great notes.   A by-product of our modern culture is that we have grown accustomed to getting our information in short doses (e.g. TV news sound bites or USA Today style newspaper articles).

Consequently, we have subconsciously trained ourselves to assimilate information better in neat little packages. If your notes are scrawled all over the paper, it fragments the flow of the information. Strive for clarity. Newspapers use a standard format to achieve clarity. Your notes can be much clearer through use of proper formatting. The *"Cornell Method"* is a very effective format described below.

> Take a sheet of loose-leaf lined notebook paper and draw a line all the way down the paper about 1-2" from the left-hand edge.

> Draw another line across the width of the paper about 1-2" up from the bottom. Repeat this process on the reverse side of the page.

Look at the highly effective result. You have ample room for notes, a left hand margin for special emphasis items or inserting supplementary data from the textbook, a large area at the bottom for a brief summary, and a little rectangular space for just about anything you want.

3. Get the concept then the details. Too often we focus on the details and don't gather an understanding of the concept. If you simply memorize dates, places, or names, you may well miss the whole point of the subject.

A good method to increase understanding is to put key concepts into your own words. If you are working from a textbook, automatically summarize each paragraph in your mind. If you are outlining text, don't simply copy the author's words; *rephrase* them in your own words. You remember your own thoughts and words much better than someone else's, and subconsciously tend to associate the important details to the core concepts.

4. Ask Why? Pull apart written material paragraph by paragraph and don't forget the captions under the illustrations.

Example: If the heading is "Stream Erosion", flip it around to read "Why do streams erode?" Then answer the questions.

If you train your mind to think in a series of questions and answers, not only will you learn more, but it also helps to lessen the test anxiety by increasing your familiarity with the question and answer process.

5. Read for reinforcement and future needs. Even if you only have 10 minutes, put your notes or a book in your hand. Your mind is similar to a computer; you have to input data in order to have it processed. *By reading, you are creating the neural connections for future retrieval.* The more times you read something, the more you reinforce the learning of ideas.

Even if you don't fully understand something on the first pass, *your mind stores much of the material for later recall.*

6. Relax to learn so go into exile. Our bodies respond to an inner clock called biorhythms. Burning the midnight oil works well for some people, but not everyone.

If possible, set aside a particular place to study that is free of distractions. Shut off the television, cell phone, and pager and exile your friends and family during your study period.

If you really are bothered by silence, try background music. Light classical music at a low volume has been shown to aid in concentration over other types. Music that evokes pleasant emotions without lyrics is highly suggested. Try just about anything by Mozart. It relaxes you.

7. Use arrows not highlighters. At best, it's difficult to read a page full of yellow, pink, blue, and green streaks. Try staring at a neon sign for a while and you'll soon see that the horde of colors obscure the message.

A quick note, a brief dash of color, an underline, and an arrow pointing to a particular passage is much clearer than a horde of highlighted words.

8. **Budget your study time.** Although you shouldn't ignore any of the material, *allocate your available study time in the same ratio that topics may appear on the test.*

Testing Tips:

1. Get smart, play dumb. Don't read anything into the question. Don't make an assumption that the test writer is looking for something else than what is asked. Stick to the question as written and don't read extra things into it.

2. Read the question and all the choices *twice* before answering the question. You may miss something by not carefully reading, and then re-reading both the question and the answers.

If you really don't have a clue as to the right answer, leave it blank on the first time through. Go on to the other questions, as they may provide a clue as to how to answer the skipped questions.

If later on, you still can't answer the skipped ones . . . ***Guess.*** The only penalty for guessing is that you *might* get it wrong. Only one thing is certain; if you don't put anything down, you will get it wrong!

3. Turn the question into a statement. Look at the way the questions are worded. The syntax of the question usually provides a clue. Does it seem more familiar as a statement rather than as a question? Does it sound strange?

By turning a question into a statement, you may be able to spot if an answer sounds right, and it may also trigger memories of material you have read.

4. Look for hidden clues. It's actually very difficult to compose multiple-foil (choice) questions without giving away part of the answer in the options presented.

In most multiple-choice questions you can often readily eliminate one or two of the potential answers. This leaves you with only two real possibilities and automatically your odds go to Fifty-Fifty for very little work.

5. Trust your instincts. For every fact that you have read, you subconsciously retain something of that knowledge. On questions that you aren't really certain about, go with your basic instincts. **Your first impression on how to answer a question is usually correct.**

6. Mark your answers directly on the test booklet. Don't bother trying to fill in the optical scan sheet on the first pass through the test.

Just be very careful not to miss-mark your answers when you eventually transcribe them to the scan sheet.

7. Watch the clock! You have a set amount of time to answer the questions. Don't get bogged down trying to answer a single question at the expense of 10 questions you can more readily answer.

THIS PAGE BLANK

SUBAREA I.   FOUNDATIONS OF SCIENTIFIC INQUIRY

COMPETENCY 1.0   UNDERSTAND THE PRINCIPLES AND PROCEDURES FOR CONDUCTING SCIENTIFIC RESEARCH.

Skill 1.1   Developing valid experimental designs for collecting data and testing hypotheses

Science may be defined as a body of knowledge that is systematically derived from study, observations, and experimentation. Its goal is to identify and establish principles and theories that may be applied to solve problems. Pseudoscience, on the other hand, is a belief that is not warranted. There is no scientific methodology or application. Some of the more classic examples of pseudoscience include astrology, the occult, and phrenology.

Scientific theory and experimentation must be repeatable. It is also possible to be disproved and is capable of change. Science depends on communication, agreement, and disagreement among scientists. It is composed of theories, laws, and hypotheses.

theory - the formation of principles or relationships which have been verified and accepted.

law - an explanation of events that occur with uniformity under the same conditions (laws of nature, law of gravitation).

hypothesis - an unproved theory or educated guess followed by research to best explain a phenomena. A theory is a proven hypothesis.

The first step in scientific inquiry is posing a question to be answered. Next, a hypothesis is formed to provide a plausible explanation. An experiment is then proposed and performed to test this hypothesis. A comparison between the predicted and observed results is the next step. Conclusions are then formed and it is determined whether the hypothesis is correct or incorrect. If incorrect, the next step is to form a new hypothesis and the process is repeated.

Skill 1.2   Recognizing the role of control groups in experiments

The procedure used to obtain data is important to the outcome. Experiments consist of controls and variables. A control is the experiment run under normal conditions. The variable includes a factor that is changed. In biology, the variable may be light, temperature, pH, time, etc. The differences in tested variables may be used to make a prediction or form a hypothesis. Only one variable should be tested at a time. For example, one would not alter both the temperature and pH of the experimental subject.

Skill 1.3   Understanding procedures for collecting and interpreting data to minimize bias

Although bias related to the investigator, the sample, the method, or the instrument may not be completely avoidable in every case, it is important to know the possible sources of bias and how bias could affect the evidence. Moreover, scientists need to be attentive to possible bias in their own work as well as that of other scientists.

Objectivity may not always be attained. However, one precaution that may be taken to guard against undetected bias is to have many different investigators or groups of investigators working on a project. By different, it is meant that the groups are made up of various nationalities, ethnic origins, ages, and political convictions and composed of both males and females. It is also important to note one's aspirations, and to make sure to be truthful to the data, even when grants, promotions, and notoriety are at risk.

For these reasons, and many more, science is a process of checks and balances. It is expected that scientific findings will be challenged, and in many cases retested. Often one experiment will be the beginning point for another. While bias does exist, the use of controlled experiments and an awareness on the part of the scientist, can go far in ensuring a sound experiment. Even if the science is well done, it may still be questioned. It is through this continual search that hypotheses are made into theories, and sometimes become laws. It is also through this search that new information is discovered.

Skill 1.4   Identifying procedures used in setting up and conducting scientific investigations in the field and in the laboratory

Light microscopes are commonly used in high school laboratory experiments. Total magnification is determined by multiplying the ocular (usually 10X) and the objective (usually 10X on low, 40X on high) lenses. Several procedures should be followed to properly care for this equipment.

-Clean all lenses with lens paper only.
-Carry microscopes with two hands; one on the arm and one on the base.
-Always begin focusing on low power, then switch to high power.
-Store microscopes with the low power objective down.
-Always use a coverslip when viewing wet mount slides.
-Bring the objective down to its lowest position then focus moving upwards to avoid breaking the slide or scratching the lens.

Wet mount slides should be made by placing a drop of water on the specimen and then putting a glass coverslip on top of the drop of water. Dropping the coverslip at a forty-five degree angle will help in avoiding air bubbles.

Chromatography uses the principles of capillarity to separate substances such as plant pigments. Molecules of a larger size will move slower up the paper, whereas smaller molecules will move more quickly producing lines of pigment.

An indicator is any substance used to assist in the classification of another substance. An example of an indicator is litmus paper. Litmus paper is a way to measure whether a substance is acidic or basic. Blue litmus turns pink when an acid is placed on it and pink litmus turns blue when a base is placed on it. pH paper is a more accurate measure of pH, with the paper turning different colors depending on the pH value.

Spectrophotometry measures percent of light at different wavelengths absorbed and transmitted by a pigment solution.

Centrifugation involves spinning substances at a high speed. The more dense part of a solution will settle to the bottom of the test tube, where the lighter material will stay on top. Centrifugation is used to separate blood into blood cells and plasma, with the heavier blood cells settling to the bottom.

Electrophoresis uses electrical charges of molecules to separate them according to their size. The molecules, such as DNA or proteins are pulled through a gel towards either the positive end of the gel box (if the material has a negative charge) or the negative end of the gel box (if the material has a positive charge). DNA is negatively charged and moves towards the positive charge.

All science labs should contain the following items of safety equipment. Those marked with an asterisk are required by state laws.

* fire blanket which is visible and accessible
*Ground Fault Circuit Interrupters (GCFI) within two feet of water supplies
*signs designating room exits
*emergency shower providing a continuous flow of water
*emergency eye wash station which can be activated by the foot or forearm
*eye protection for every student and a means of sanitizing equipment
*emergency exhaust fans providing ventilation to the outside of the building
*master cut-off switches for gas, electric and compressed air. Switches must have
  permanently attached handles. Cut-off switches must be clearly labeled.
*an ABC fire extinguisher
*storage cabinets for flammable materials
*chemical spill control kit
*fume hood with a motor which is spark proof
*protective laboratory aprons made of flame retardant material
*signs which will alert potential hazardous conditions
*labeled containers for broken glassware, flammables, corrosives, and
  waste.

Students should wear safety goggles when performing dissections, heating, or while using acids and bases. Hair should always be tied back and objects should never be placed in the mouth. Food should not be consumed while in the laboratory. Hands should always be washed before and after laboratory experiments. In case of an accident, eye washes and showers should be used for eye contamination or a chemical spill that covers the student's body. Small chemical spills should only be contained and cleaned by the teacher. Kitty litter or a chemical spill kit should be used to clean spills. For large spills, the school administration and the local fire department should be notified. Biological spills should also be handled only by the teacher. Contamination with biological waste can be cleaned by using bleach when appropriate.

Accidents and injuries should always be reported to the school administration and local health facilities. The severity of the accident or injury will determine the course of action to pursue.

It is the responsibility of the teacher to provide a safe environment for their students. Proper supervision greatly reduces the risk of injury and a teacher should never leave a class for any reason without providing alternate supervision. After an accident, two factors are considered; foreseeability and negligence. Foreseeability is the anticipation that an event may occur under certain circumstances. Negligence is the failure to exercise ordinary or reasonable care. Safety procedures should be a part of the science curriculum and a well managed classroom is important to avoid potential lawsuits.

Skill 1.5   Recognizing variables being held constant, being manipulated (i.e., independent variables), and responding (i.e., dependent variables)

An independent variable is one that is changed or manipulated by the researcher. This could be the amount of light given to a plant or the temperature at which bacteria is grown. The dependent variable is that which is influenced by the independent variable; it responds to the independent variable. If there are multiple variables, and you choose to study only one, then the variables unchanged are said to be held constant. For example, you might study multiple objects, each with the same size and shape (volume is constant), but differing in density.

Skill 1.6   Identifying the most effective method for presenting data for a given purpose (e.g., graph, table, map)

The type of graphic representation used to display observations depends on the data that is collected. Line graphs are used to compare different sets of related data or to predict data that has not yet be measured. An example of a line graph would be comparing the rate of activity of different enzymes at varying temperatures. A bar graph or histogram is used to compare different items and make comparisons based on this data. An example of a bar graph would be comparing the ages of children in a classroom. A pie chart is useful when organizing data as part of a whole. A good use for a pie chart would be displaying the percent of time students spend on various after school activities.

As noted before, the independent variable is controlled by the experimenter. This variable is placed on the x-axis (horizontal axis). The dependent variable is influenced by the independent variable and is placed on the y-axis (vertical axis). It is important to choose the appropriate units for labeling the axes. It is best to take the largest value to be plotted and divide it by the number of block, and rounding to the nearest whole number.

Skill 1.7   Evaluating simple descriptive statistics

Simple descriptive statistics are meant to describe features of data in a study. This is a description of what was observed or what the data shows. It is not meant to infer anything further, nor does it speculate about what may be. Descriptive Statistics are used to present quantitative descriptions in a manageable form.   Consider the infamous the Grade Point Average (GPA). The single number assigned describes a large number of grades, one per each class ever taken. The GPA describes the general performance of the student. While condensing large amounts of information, the danger in descriptive statistics is that the whole picture can become less clear. For example, we don't know if the student had a high GPA because s/he took relatively easy courses, or if the student never took a biology class in their whole collegiate career. There is potentially a wider range of experiences than is encompassed in a descriptive statistic. One should keep this in mind when evaluating a situation or material when only a simple descriptive statistic is provided.

Skill 1.8   Interpreting data presented in different formats

Data collected is initially organized into tables. Trends or patterns in data can be difficult to identify using tables of numbers. However, more often than not, the data is compiled into graphs. Graphs help scientists visualize and interpret the variation in data. Depending on the nature of the data, there are many types of graphs. Bar graphs, pie charts and line graphs are just a few methods used to pictorially represent numerical data. There are six basic types of graphs.

Column Graphs

Column graphs consist of patterned rectangles displayed along a baseline called the x-category or the horizontal axis. The height of the rectangle represents the amount of data. Column graphs best show:
• changes in data over time (short time series)
• comparisons of several items (relationship between two series)

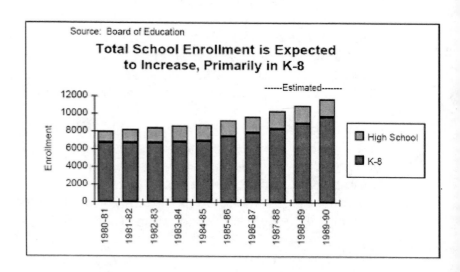

BIOLOGY   6

Bar Graphs
Column graphs can be described as rectangles that are arranged horizontally. The length of each rectangle represents its value. Bar graphs are sometimes referred to as histograms. Bar graphs best show:
• data series with no natural order.

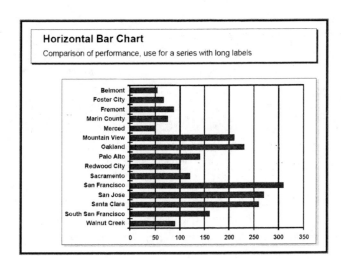

Bar graphs are good for looking at differences amongst similar things. If the data are a time series, a carefully chosen column graph is generally more appropriate but bar graphs can be used to vary a presentation when many column graphs of time series are used. One advantage of bar graphs is that there is greater horizontal space for variable descriptors because the vertical axis is the category axis.

Line Graphs
Line graphs show data points connected by lines; different series are given different line markings (for example, dashed or dotted) or different tick marks. Line graphs are useful when the data points are more important than the transitions between them. They best show:
• the comparison of long series
• a general trend is the message.
Line graphs are good for showing trends or changes over time.

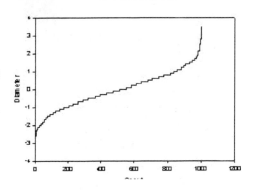

Pie Charts
A pie chart is a circle with radii connecting the center to the edge. The area between two radii is called a slice. Data values are proportionate to the angle between the radii. Pie charts best show:
• parts of a whole
Be careful of too many slices since they result in a cluttered graph. Six slices is the general rule as to how many slices can be handled on one pie.

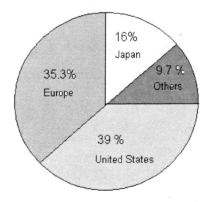

BIOLOGY

7

Area Graphs

Area charts show the relative contributions over time that each data series makes to a whole picture and are "stacked line graphs" in the sense that values are added to the variables below. Unlike line graphs, the space between lines is filled with shadings. Area graphs are similar to line graphs with the added drama of shading between lines to

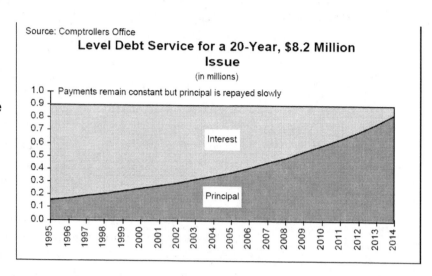

emphasize variation between whatever the lines represent. They differ from line graphs in that the shaded areas are "added" one on top of the next. Thus, the scale provides accurate measurements only for the lowest part of the graph. This can cause misinterpretation if not fully understood. If reasonable, consider putting the "flattest" graph on the bottom.

Scatter Graphs

A scatter plot is the simplest type of graph. It simply plots the data points against their values, without adding an connecting lines, bars or other stuff. The first variable is measured along the x-axis and the second along the y-axis. Because of this, scatter graphs do not have descriptors in the same sense as other graphs.

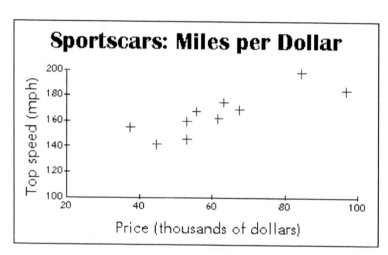

Scatter graphs best show possible relationships between two variables. The purpose of the graph is to try to decide if some partial or indirect relationship—a correlation—exists.

Skill 1.9   Evaluating the validity of conclusions; and assessing the reliability of sources of information

Because people often attempt to use scientific evidence in support of political or personal agendas, the ability to evaluate the credibility of scientific claims is a necessary skill in today's society. In evaluating scientific claims made in the media, public debates, and advertising, one should follow several guidelines.

First, scientific, peer-reviewed journals are the most accepted source for information on scientific experiments and studies. One should carefully scrutinize any claim that does not reference peer-reviewed literature.

Second, the media and those with an agenda to advance (advertisers, debaters, etc.) often overemphasize the certainty and importance of experimental results. One should question any scientific claim that sounds fantastical or overly certain.

Finally, knowledge of experimental design and the scientific method is important in evaluating the credibility of studies. For example, one should look for the inclusion of control groups and the presence of data to support the given conclusions.

COMPETENCY 2.0 APPLY KNOWLEDGE OF METHODS AND MATERIALS USED IN SCIENTIFIC INVESTIGATIONS.

Skill 2.1 Identifying procedures and sources of information (e.g., MSDS sheets, chemical hygiene plans) for the safe use and storage of materials related to scientific investigations (e.g., chemicals, biohazards, equipment)

All laboratory solutions should be prepared as directed in the lab manual. Care should be taken to avoid contamination. All glassware should be rinsed thoroughly with distilled water before using and cleaned well after use. All solutions should be made with distilled water as tap water contains dissolved particles that may affect the results of an experiment. Unused solutions should be disposed of according to local disposal procedures.

The "Right to Know Law" covers science teachers who work with potentially hazardous chemicals. Briefly, the law states that employees must be informed of potentially toxic chemicals. An inventory must be made available if requested. The inventory must contain information about the hazards and properties of the chemicals. This inventory is to be checked against the "Substance List". Training must be provided on the safe handling and interpretation of the Material Safety Data Sheet.

The following chemicals are potential carcinogens and are not allowed in school facilities: Acrylonitriel, Arsenic compounds, Asbestos, Bensidine, Benzene, Cadmium compounds, Chloroform, Chromium compounds, Ethylene oxide, Ortho-toluidine, Nickel powder, and Mercury.

Chemicals should not be stored on bench tops or on heat sources. They should be stored in groups based on their reactivity with one another and in protective storage cabinets. All containers within the lab must be labeled. Suspect and known carcinogens must be labeled as such and segregated within trays to contain leaks and spills.

Chemical waste should be disposed of in properly labeled containers. Waste should be separated based on their reactivity with other chemicals.

Biological material should never be stored near food or water used for human consumption. All biological material should be appropriately labeled. All blood and body fluids should be put in a well-contained container with a secure lid to prevent leaking. All biological waste should be disposed of in biological hazardous waste bags.

Material safety data sheets are available for every chemical and biological substance. These are available directly from the company of acquisition or the internet. The manuals for equipment used in the lab should be read and understood before using them.

Skill 2.2 Understanding the practices and requirements related to the handling and ethical use of living organisms

No dissections may be performed on living mammalian vertebrates or birds. Lower order life and invertebrates may be used. Biological experiments may be done with all animals except mammalian vertebrates or birds. No physiological harm may result to the animal. All animals housed and cared for in the school must be handled in a safe and humane manner. Animals are not to remain on school premises during extended vacations unless adequate care is provided. Any instructor who intentionally refuses to comply with the laws may be suspended or dismissed.

Pathogenic organisms must never be used for experimentation. Students should adhere to the following rules at all times when working with microorganisms to avoid accidental contamination:

1. Treat all microorganisms as if they were pathogenic.
2. Maintain sterile conditions at all times

Animals that are not obtained from recognized sources should not be used. Decaying animals or those of unknown origin may harbor pathogens and/or parasites. Specimens should be rinsed before handling. Latex gloves are desirable. If not available, students with sores or scratches should be excused from the activity. Formaldehyde is likely carcinogenic and should be avoided or disposed of according to district regulations. Students objecting to dissections for moral reasons should be given an alternative assignment. Interactive dissections are available online or from software companies for those students who object to performing dissections. There should be no penalty for those students who refuse to physically perform a dissection.

Skill 2.3 Applying procedures for selecting and using measurement devices (e.g., rulers, balance scales, thermometers)

Science uses the metric system; as it is accepted worldwide and allows easier comparison among experiments done by scientists around the world.

The meter is the basic metric unit of length. One meter is 1.1 yards. The liter is the basic metric unit of volume. One (1) gallon is 3.846 liters. The gram is the basic metric unit of mass. 1000 grams is 2.2 pounds.

The following prefixes are used to describe the multiples of the basic metric units.

deca- 10X the base unit   deci - 1/10 the base unit
hecto- 100X the base unit   centi - 1/100 the base unit
kilo- 1,000X the base unit   milli - 1/1,000 the base unit
mega- 1,000,000X the base unit   micro- 1/1,000,000 the base unit
giga- 1,000,000,000X the base unit   nano- 1/1,000,000,000 the base unit
tera- 1,000,000,000,000X the base unit   pico- 1/1,000,000,000,000 the base unit

The common instrument used for measuring volume is the graduated cylinder. The unit of measurement is usually in milliliters (mL). It is important for accurate measure to read the liquid in the cylinder at the bottom of the meniscus, the curved surface of the liquid.

The common instrument used is measuring mass is the triple beam balance. The triple beam balance is measured in as low as tenths of a gram and can be estimated to the hundredths of a gram.

The ruler or meter sticks are the most commonly used instruments for measuring length. Measurements in science should always be measured in metric units. Be sure when measuring length that the metric units are used.

COMPETENCY 3.0 UNDERSTAND THE NATURE AND HISTORY OF SCIENTIFIC THOUGHT AND INQUIRY.

Skill 3.1 Being aware of the reliance of scientific inquiry on empirical data, verifiable evidence, and logical reasoning

Observations, however general they may seem, lead scientists to create a viable question and an educated guess (hypothesis) about what to expect. While scientists often have laboratories set up to study a specific thing, it is likely that along the way they will find an unexpected result. It is always important to be open-minded and to look at all of the information. An open-minded approach to science provides room for more questioning, and, hence, more learning.

A central concept in science is that all evidence is empirical. This means that all evidence must be is observed by the five senses. The studied phenomenon must be both observable and measurable, with reproducible results. The question stage of scientific inquiry involves repetition. By repeating the experiment you can discover whether or not you have reproducibility. If results are reproducible, the hypothesis is valid. If the results are not reproducible, one has more questions to ask.

Armed with knowledge of the subject matter, students can effectively conduct investigations. They need to learn to think critically and logically to connect evidence with explanations. This includes deciding what evidence should be used and accounting for unusual data. Based upon data collected during experimentation, basic statistical analysis, and measures of probability can be used to make predictions and develop interpretations.

Students should be able to review the data, summarize, and form a logical argument about the cause-and-effect relationships. It is important to differentiate between causes and effects and determine when causality is uncertain.

When developing proposed explanations, the students should be able to express their level of confidence in the proposed explanations and point out possible sources of uncertainty and error. When formulating explanations, it is important to distinguish between error and unanticipated results. Possible sources of error would include assumptions of models and measuring techniques or devices.

With confidence in the proposed explanations, the students need to identify what would be required to reject the proposed explanations. Based upon their experience, they should develop new questions to promote further inquiry.

Skill 3.2   Recognizing the limits of science

Science is limited by the available technology. An example of this would be the relationship of the discovery of the cell and the invention of the microscope. As our technology improves, more hypotheses will become theories and possibly laws. Science is also limited by the data that is able to be collected. Data may be interpreted differently on different occasions. Science limitations cause explanations to be changeable as new technologies emerge.

Skill 3.3   Evaluating the effect of researcher bias on scientific investigations and the interpretation of data

Scientific research can be biased in the choice of what data to consider, in the reporting or recording of the data, and/or in how the data are interpreted. The scientist's emphasis may be influenced by his/her nationality, sex, ethnic origin, age, or political convictions. For example, when studying a group of animals, male scientists may focus on the social behavior of the males and typically male characteristics.

Although bias related to the investigator, the sample, the method, or the instrument may not be completely avoidable in every case, it is important to know the possible sources of bias and how bias could affect the evidence. Moreover, scientists need to be attentive to possible bias in their own work as well as that of other scientists.

Skill 3.4   Demonstrating an awareness of the contributions made in biology by individuals of diverse backgrounds

Curiosity is the heart of science. Maybe this is why so many diverse people are drawn to it. In the area of zoology one of the most recognized scientists is Jane Goodall. Miss Goodall is known for her research with chimpanzees in Africa. Jane has spent many years abroad conducting long term studies of chimp interactions, and returns from Africa to lecture and provide information about Africa, the chimpanzees, and her institute located in Tanzania.

In the area of chemistry we recognize Dorothy Crowfoot Hodgkin. She studied at Oxford and won the Nobel Prize of Chemistry in 1964 for recognizing the shape of vitamin B-12.

Have you ever heard of Florence Nightingale? She was a true person living in the 1800's and she shaped the nursing profession. Florence was born into wealth and shocked her family by choosing to study health reforms for the poor in lieu of attending the expected social events. Florence studied nursing in Paris and became involved in the Crimean war. The British lacked supplies and the secretary of war asked for Florence's assistance. She earned her nickname walking the floors at night checking on patients and writing letters to British officials demanding supplies.

In 1903 the Nobel Prize in Physics was jointly awarded to three individuals: Marie Curie, Pierre Curie, and Becquerel. Marie was the first woman ever to receive this prestigious award. In addition, she received the Nobel Prize in chemistry in 1911, making her the only person to receive two Nobel awards in science. Ironically, her cause of death in 1934 was of overexposure to radioactivity, the research for which she was so respected.

Neil Armstrong is an American icon. He will always be symbolically linked to our aeronautics program. This astronaut and naval aviator is known for being the first human to set foot on the Moon.

Sir Alexander Fleming was a pharmacologist from Scotland who isolated the antibiotic penicillin from a fungus in 1928. Flemming also noted that bacteria developed resistance whenever too little penicillin was used or when it was used for too short a period, a key problem we still face today.

Anton van Leeuwenhoek is known as the father of microscopy. In the 1650s, Leeuwenhoek began making tiny lenses which gave magnifications up to 300x. He was the first to see and describe bacteria, yeast plants, and the microscopic life found in water. Over the years, light microscopes have advanced to produce greater clarity and magnification. The scanning electron microscope (SEM) was developed in the 1950s. Instead of light, a beam of electrons passes through the specimen. Scanning electron microscopes have a resolution about one thousand times greater than light microscopes. The disadvantage of the SEM is that the chemical and physical methods used to prepare the sample result in the death of the specimen.

In the late 1800s, Pasteur discovered the role of microorganisms in the cause of disease, pasteurization, and the rabies vaccine. Koch took this observations one step further by formulating that specific diseases were caused by specific pathogens. Koch's postulates are still used as guidelines in the field of microbiology: the same pathogen must be found in every diseased person, the pathogen must be isolated and grown in culture, the disease is induced in experimental animals from the culture, and the same pathogen must be isolated from the experimental animal.

DNA structure was another key event in biological study. In the 1950s, James Watson and Francis Crick discovered the structure of a DNA molecule as that of a double helix. This structure made it possible to explain DNA's ability to replicate and to control the synthesis of proteins.

It is important to realize that many of the most complex scientific questions have been answered in a collaborative form. The human genome project is a great example of research conducted and shared by multiple countries world wide. It is also interesting to note that because of differing cultural beliefs, some cultures may be more likely to allow areas of research that other cultures may be unlikely to examine.

Skill 3.5   Analyzing the dynamic nature of scientific knowledge, including ways in which scientific knowledge is acquired, modified, and disseminated

Scientific knowledge happens through use of the scientific method. Science investigation is a very important part of science. Science investigation consists of a number of steps designed to solve a problem. This is important because it helps in solving scientific problems and to gather new information. Scientists start with a problem and solve it in an orderly fashion called the scientific method. This is made up of a series of steps, which, when applied properly, solve scientific problems. The key to the success of this method lies in minimizing human prejudice. As human beings, we tend to have bias. The steps consist of identifying the problem, gathering information, formulating a hypothesis, experimental design, interpreting data, and drawing conclusions.

The first step in a science investigation is identifying the problem. As we observe, we notice interesting things that arouse our curiosity. We ask ourselves the basic questions of enquiry – how, why, what, when, which and where. The two most important questions are how and why. We can classify observations into two types. The first is qualitative, which we describe in words. No mention of numbers or quantities is made – the water is very hot, the solution is sour, etc. The second type is quantitative, where numbers and quantities are used. This format is more precise –mass: 125 kg., distance: 500 km, etc.

The second step is gathering information. As information as possible is collected from various sources like internet, books, journals, knowledgeable people, newspapers etc. This lays a solid foundation for formulating a hypothesis.

The third step is hypothesizing. This is making statement about the problem with the knowledge acquired and using the two important words, 'if' and 'when'.

The next step is designing an experiment. Before this is done, we need to identify the control, the constants, the independent variables and the dependent variable.

For beginners, the simplest investigation would be to manipulate only one variable at a time. In this way, the experiment doesn't get too complicated and is easier to handle. The control has to be identified and then the variable which can effect the outcome of the results. For an experiment to be authentic and reliable, constants have to be identified and kept constant throughout the experiment. Finally, the dependent variable, which is dependent on the independent variable, has to be identified. The dependent variable is the factor that is being measured in an experiment – e.g. height of plant, number of leaves, etc. For an experiment to be successful, it should be completed in 10-12 days. The results are noted carefully. At the end of the experiment, the data have to be analyzed and searched for patterns. Any science investigation has to be repeated at least twice to get reproducible results. After the analysis, conclusions must be drawn based on the data.

In order to draw conclusions, we need to study the data on hand. The data tell us whether or not the hypothesis is correct. If the hypothesis is not correct, another hypothesis has to be formulated and an experiment has to be done.

If the hypothesis is tested and the results are repeated in further experimentation, a theory could be formulated. A theory is a hypothesis that is tested repeatedly by different scientists and has yielded the same results. A theory has more validity because it could be used to predict future events.

Scientific inquiries should end in formulating an explanation or model. Models should be physical, conceptual, and mathematical. While drawing conclusions, a lot of discussion and arguments are generated. There may be several possible explanations for any given sets of results: not all of them are reasonable. Carefully evaluating and analyzing the data creates a reasonable conclusion. The conclusion needs to be backed up by scientific criteria.

After the conclusion is drawn, the final step is communication. In this age, much emphasis is put on the method of communication. The conclusions must be communicated by clearly describing the information using accurate data, visual presentation like graphs (bar/line/pie), tables/charts, diagrams, artwork, and other appropriate media like power point presentation. Modern technology must be used whenever it is necessary. The method of communication must be suitable to the audience.

Written communication is as important as oral communication. This is essential for submitting research papers to scientific journals, newspapers, other magazines etc.

COMPETENCY 4.0   UNDERSTAND THE RELATIONSHIP OF BIOLOGY TO CONTEMPORARY, HISTORICAL, TECHNOLOGICAL, AND SOCIETAL ISSUES.

Skill 4.1   Demonstrate an awareness of the differences between science and technology

Biological science is closely connected to technology and the other sciences and greatly impacts society and everyday life. Scientific discoveries often lead to technological advances and, conversely, technology is often necessary for scientific investigation and advances in technology often expand the reach of scientific discoveries. In addition, biology and the other scientific disciplines share several unifying concepts and processes that help unify the study of science. Finally, because biology is the science of living systems, biology directly impacts society and everyday life.

Science and technology, while distinct fields, are closely related. Science attempts to investigate and explain the natural world, while technology attempts to solve human adaptation problems. Technology often results from the application of scientific discoveries, and advances in technology can increase the impact of scientific discoveries. For example, Watson and Crick used science to discover the structure of DNA and their discovery led to many biotechnological advances in the manipulation of DNA. These technological advances greatly influenced the medical and pharmaceutical fields. The success of Watson and Crick's experiments, however, was dependent on the technology available. Without the necessary technology, the experiments would have failed.

Skill 4.2   Analyzing historical, political, and social factors affecting developments in biology, including current societal issues related to developments in biology and technology

Society as a whole impacts biological research. The pressure from the majority of society has led to these bans and restrictions on human cloning research. Human cloning has been restricted in the United States and many other countries. The U.S. legislature has banned the use of federal funds for the development of human cloning techniques. Some individual states have banned human cloning regardless of where the funds originate.

The demand for genetically modified crops by society and industry has steadily increased over the years. Genetic engineering in the agricultural field has led to improved crops for human use and consumption. Crops are genetically modified for increased growth and insect resistance because of the demand for larger and greater quantities of produce.

With advances in biotechnology come those in society who oppose it. Ethical questions come into play when discussing animal and human research. Does it need to be done? What are the effects on humans and animals? There are no right or wrong answers to these questions. There are governmental agencies in place to regulate the use of humans and animals for research.

Science and technology are often referred to as a "double-edged sword". Although advances in medicine have greatly improved the quality and length of life, certain moral and ethical controversies have arisen. Unforeseen environmental problems may result from technological advances. Advances in science have led to an improved economy through biotechnology as applied to agriculture, yet it has put our health care system at risk and has caused the cost of medical care to skyrocket. Society depends on science, yet is necessary that the public be scientifically literate and informed in order to allow potentially unethical procedures to occur. Especially vulnerable are the areas of genetic research and fertility. It is important for science teachers to stay abreast of current research and to involve students in critical thinking and ethics whenever possible.

The use of animals in biological research has expedited many scientific discoveries. Animal research has allowed scientists to learn more about animal biological systems, including the circulatory and reproductive systems. One significant use of animals is for the testing of drugs, vaccines, and other products (such as perfumes and shampoos) before use or consumption by humans. Along with the pros of animal research, the cons are also very significant. The debate about the ethical treatment of animals has been ongoing since the introduction of animals in research. Many people believe the use of animals in research is cruel and unnecessary. Animal use is federally and locally regulated. The purpose of the Institutional Animal Care and Use Committee (IACUC) is to oversee and evaluate all aspects of an institution's animal care and use program.

Skill 4.3   Recognizing ethical issues related to biological research (e.g., cloning, genetic engineering)

Genetic engineering has drastically advanced the biotechnology. With these advancements come concerns for safety and ethical questions. Many safety concerns have answered by strict government regulations. The FDA, USDA, EPA, and National Institutes of Health are just a few of the government agencies that regulate pharmaceutical, food, and environmental technology advancements.

Cloning: Cloning is to derive a population of cells from a single cell. There are different types of cloning and the technology for cloning could be used for other purposes as well. There are three main types of cloning.

In 2001, the first human embryo was cloned for the purpose of advancing therapeutic research by scientists from Advanced Cell technologies (ACT). To do this, scientists collected eggs from women's ovaries and then removed the genetic material from these eggs with a very fine needle and then a skin cell was inserted inside the enucleated egg to serve as a new nucleus. The egg began to divide after it was stimulated by ionomycin. The success in these experiments was very limited.

Cloning technologies are useful in learning about gene therapy, genetic engineering of organisms, and genome sequencing. Some of the risks of cloning are that the reproductive cloning is very expensive and highly inefficient. There may be errors while DNA duplicates inside a host cell.

Physicians from the American Medical Association and scientists with the American Association for the Advancement of Science have issued formal statements advising against human reproductive cloning.

Several ethical questions arise when discussing biotechnology. Should embryonic stem cell research be allowed? Is animal testing humane? These are just a couple of ethical questions that every person wonders. There are strong arguments for both sides of the issues and there are some government regulations in place to monitor these issues.

Skill 4.4 Evaluating the credibility of scientific claims made in various forums (e.g., the popular media, professional journals, advertising)

Because people often attempt to use scientific evidence in support of political or personal agendas, the ability to evaluate the credibility of scientific claims is a necessary skill in today's society. In evaluating scientific claims made in the media, public debates, and advertising, one should follow several guidelines.

First, scientific, peer-reviewed journals are the most accepted source for information on scientific experiments and studies. One should carefully scrutinize any claim that does not reference peer-reviewed literature.

Second, the media and those with an agenda to advance (advertisers, debaters, etc.) often overemphasize the certainty and importance of experimental results. One should question any scientific claim that sounds fantastical or overly certain.

Finally, knowledge of experimental design and the scientific method is important in evaluating the credibility of studies. For example, one should look for the inclusion of control groups and the presence of data to support the given conclusions.

COMPETENCY 5.0   UNDERSTAND INTERRELATIONSHIPS AMONG THE LIFE, PHYSICAL, AND EARTH/SPACE SCIENCES AND AMONG SCIENCE, MATHEMATICS, AND TECHNOLOGY.

Skill 5.1   Recognizing major unifying themes and concepts in the various scientific disciplines (e.g., classification, cause and effect, conservation of energy, entropy)

The following are the concepts and processes generally recognized as common to all scientific disciplines:

- Systems, order, and organization
- Evidence, models, and explanation
- Constancy, change, and measurement
- Evolution and equilibrium
- Form and function

Systems, order, and organization

Because the natural world is so complex, the study of science involves the **organization** of items into smaller groups based on interaction or interdependence. These groups are called **systems**. Examples of organization are the periodic table of elements and the five-kingdom classification scheme for living organisms. Examples of systems are the solar system, cardiovascular system, Newton's laws of force and motion, and the laws of conservation.

Order refers to the behavior and measurability of organisms and events in nature. The arrangement of planets in the solar system and the life cycle of bacterial cells are examples of order.

Evidence, models, and explanations

Scientists use **evidence** and **models** to form **explanations** of natural events. Models are miniaturized representations of a larger event or system. Evidence is anything that furnishes proof.

Constancy, change, and measurement

Constancy and **change** describe the observable properties of natural organisms and events. Scientists use different systems of **measurement** to observe change and constancy. For example, the freezing and melting points of given substances and the speed of sound are constant under constant conditions. Growth, decay, and erosion are all examples of natural change.

Evolution and equilibrium

Evolution is the process of change over a long period of time. While biological evolution is the most common example, one can also classify technological advancement, changes in the universe, and changes in the environment as evolution.

Equilibrium is the state of balance between opposing forces of change. Homeostasis and ecological balance are examples of equilibrium.

Form and function

Form and **function** are properties of organisms and systems that are closely related. The function of an object usually dictates its form and the form of an object usually facilitates its function. For example, the form of the heart (e.g. muscle, valves) allows it to perform its function of circulating blood through the body.

Skill 5.2   Understanding the interdisciplinary connections among science, mathematics, and technology and their applications in real-world contexts

Math, science, and technology have common themes in how they are applied and understood. All three use models, diagrams, and graphs to simplify a concept for analysis and interpretation. Patterns observed in these systems lead to predictions based on these observations. Another common theme among these three systems is equilibrium. Equilibrium is a state in which forces are balanced, resulting in stability. Static equilibrium is stability due to a lack of changes and dynamic equilibrium is stability due to a balance between opposite forces.

SUBAREA II.   **CELLULAR FUNCTION**

COMPETENCY 6.0   **UNDERSTAND CELL THEORY AND CELLULAR STRUCTURE AND FUNCTION.**

Skill 6.1   **Recognizing the basic tenets of cell theory**

Cell theory has been an evolution of sorts. It was begun by Dutrochet in 1824. He stated that "the cell is the fundamental element in the structure of living bodies…". Robert Brown was the first scientist to report seeing biological processes within a cell. Later, Theodore Schwann would be the first to coin the term cell theory. Schwann insisted that plants were made of cells and Schlieden declared that animals were composed of cells. Science has continued to evolve since then, and our technologies have improved. It was Louis Pasteur's work focusing on microbes that proved the cell theory. We can now use electron microscopes to watch cells reproduce and metabolize. The cell is considered to be the smallest structure in biology that has all the properties of living things. Current cell theory includes the following:

1. The cell is the basic unit of an organism.
2. Organisms are made up of one (or more) cells.
3. Cells originate from pre-existing cells through division.
4. Cells carry genetic material passed to daughter cells during cellular division.
6. Metabolism occurs within cells.

Skill 6.2   **Comparing prokaryotic (i.e., archaea, eubacteria) and eukaryotic cells**

The cell is the basic unit of all living things. There are three types of cells. They are prokaryotes, eukaryotes, and archaea. Archaea have some similarities with prokaryotes, but are as distantly related to prokaryotes as prokaryotes are to eukaryotes.

PROKARYOTES

Prokaryotes consist only of bacteria and cyanobacteria (formerly known as blue-green algae). The classification of prokaryotes is in the diagram below.

Prokaryotes (Monera)

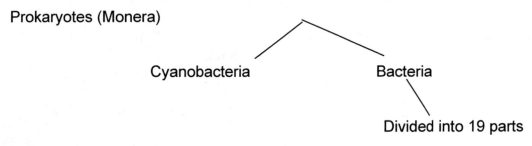

Cyanobacteria   Bacteria

Divided into 19 parts

BIOLOGY

These cells have no defined nucleus or nuclear membrane. The DNA, RNA, and ribosomes float freely within the cell. The cytoplasm has a single chromosome condensed to form a nucleoid. Prokaryotes have a thick cell wall made up of amino sugars (glycoproteins). This is for protection, to give the cell shape, and to keep the cell from bursting. It is the cell wall of bacteria that is targeted by the antibiotic penicillin. Penicillin works by disrupting the cell wall, thus killing the cell.

The cell wall surrounds the cell membrane (plasma membrane). The cell membrane consists of a lipid bilayer that controls the passage of molecules in and out of the cell. Some prokaryotes have a capsule made of polysaccharides that surrounds the cell wall for extra protection from higher organisms.

Many bacterial cells have appendages used for movement called flagella. Some cells also have pili, which are a protein strand used for attachment of the bacteria. Pili may also be used for sexual conjugation (where the DNA from one bacterial cell is transferred to another bacterial cell).

Prokaryotes are the most numerous and widespread organisms on earth. Bacteria were most likely the first cells and date back in the fossil record to 3.5 billion years ago. Their ability to adapt to the environment allows them to thrive in a wide variety of habitats.

EUKARYOTES

Eukaryotic cells are found in protists, fungi, plants, and animals. Most eukaryotic cells are larger than prokaryotic cells. They contain many organelles, which are membrane bound areas for specific functions. Their cytoplasm contains a cytoskeleton that provides a protein framework for the cell. The cytoplasm also supports the organelles and contains the ions and molecules necessary for cell function. The cytoplasm is contained by the plasma membrane. The plasma membrane allows molecules to pass in and out of the cell. The membrane can bud inward to engulf outside material in a process called endocytosis. Exocytosis is a secretory mechanism, the reverse of endocytosis.

The most significant differentiation between prokaryotes and eukaryotes is that eukaryotes have a nucleus.

ARCHAEA

There are three kinds of organisms with archaea cells: methanogens are obligate anaerobes that produce methane, halobacteria can live only in concentrated brine solutions, and thermoacidophiles can only live in acidic hot springs.

EUBACTERIA VS. ARCHAEBACTERIA

Archaebacteria and eubacteria are the two main branches of prokaryotic (moneran) evolution. Archaebacteria evolved from the earliest cells. Most achaebacteria inhabit extreme environments. There are three main groups of archaebacteria. Methanogens are strict anaerobes, extreme halophiles live in high salt concentrations, and extreme thermophiles live in hot temperatures (hot springs).

Most prokaryotes fall into the eubacteria (bacteria) domain. Bacteria are divided according to their morphology (shape). Bacilli are rod shaped bacteria, cocci are round bacteria and spirilli are spiral shaped.

The Gram stain is a procedure used to differentiate the cell wall make-up of bacteria. Gram positive bacteria have simple cell walls consisting of large amounts of peptidoglycan. These bacteria pick up the stain, revealing a purple color when observed under the microscope. Gram negative bacteria have a more complex cell wall consisting of less peptidoglycan, but have large amounts of lipopolysaccharides. The lipopolysaccharides resist the stain, revealing a pink color when observed under the microscope. Because of the lipopolysaccharide cell wall, Gram negative bacteria tend to be more toxic and are more resistant to antibiotics and host defense mechanisms.

Bacteria reproduce by binary fission. This asexual process is simply dividing the bacterium in half. All new organisms are exact clones of the parent.

Some bacteria have a sticky capsule that protects the cell wall and is also used for adhesion to surfaces. Pili are surface appendages for adhesion to other cells.

Bacteria locomotion is via flagella or taxis. Taxis is the movement towards or away from a stimulus. The methods for obtaining nutrition are: for photosynthetic organisms or producers- the conversion of sunlight to chemical energy, consumers or heterotrophs- consuming other living organisms, and saprophytes are consumers that live off dead or decaying material.

In comparison, archaebacteria contain no peptidoglycan in the cell wall, they are not inhibited by antibiotics, they have several kinds of RNA polymerase, and they do not have a nuclear envelope. Eubacteria (bacteria) have peptidoglycan in the cell wall, they are susceptible to antibiotics, they have one kind of RNA polymerase, and they have no nuclear envelope.

Skill 6.3 **Recognizing the structures, functions, and interactions of cellular components common to all cells (e.g., membranes, metabolism, genetic information) and those that are unique to some cells (e.g., nucleus, lysosomes, chloroplasts)**

The nucleus is the brain of the cell that contains all of the cell's genetic information. The chromosomes consist of chromatin, which is a complex of DNA and proteins. The chromosomes are tightly coiled to conserve space while providing a large surface area. The nucleus is the site of transcription of the DNA into RNA. The nucleolus is where ribosomes are made. There is at least one of these dark-staining bodies inside the nucleus of most eukaryotes. The nuclear envelope is two membranes separated by a narrow space. The envelope contains many pores that let RNA out of the nucleus.

Ribosomes are the site for protein synthesis. Ribosomes may be free floating in the cytoplasm or attached to the endoplasmic reticulum. There may be up to a half a million ribosomes in a cell, depending on how much protein is made by the cell.

The endoplasmic reticulum (ER) is folded and provides a large surface area. It is the "roadway" of the cell and allows for transport of materials through and out of the cell. There are two types of ER. Smooth endoplasmic reticulum contains no ribosomes on their surface. This is the site of lipid synthesis. Rough endoplasmic reticulum has ribosomes on their surface. They aid in the synthesis of proteins that are membrane bound or destined for secretion.

Many of the products made in the ER proceed on to the Golgi apparatus. The Golgi apparatus functions to sort, modify, and package molecules that are made in the other parts of the cell (like the ER). These molecules are either sent out of the cell or to other organelles within the cell. The Golgi apparatus is a stacked structure to increase the surface area.

Lysosomes are found mainly in animal cells. These contain digestive enzymes that break down food, substances not needed, viruses, damaged cell components and eventually the cell itself. It is believed that lysomomes are responsible for the aging process.

Mitochondria are large organelles that are the site of cellular respiration, where ATP is made to supply energy to the cell. Muscle cells have many mitochondria because they use a great deal of energy. Mitochondria have their own DNA, RNA, and ribosomes and are capable of reproducing by binary fission if there is a greater demand for additional energy. Mitochondria have two membranes: a smooth outer membrane and a folded inner membrane. The folds inside the mitochondria are called cristae. They provide a large surface area for cellular respiration to occur.

Plastids are found only in photosynthetic organisms. They are similar to the mitochondria due to the double membrane structure. They also have their own DNA, RNA, and ribosomes and can reproduce if the need for the increased capture of sunlight becomes necessary. There are several types of plastids. Chloroplasts are the sight of photosynthesis. The stroma is the chloroplast's inner membrane space. The stoma encloses sacs called thylakoids that contain the photosynthetic pigment chlorophyll. The chlorophyll traps sunlight inside the thylakoid to generate ATP which is used in the stroma to produce carbohydrates and other products. The chromoplasts make and store yellow and orange pigments. They provide color to leaves, flowers, and fruits. The amyloplasts store starch and are used as a food reserve. They are abundant in roots like potatoes.

The Endosymbiotic Theory states that mitochondria and chloroplasts were once free living and possibly evolved from prokaryotic cells. At some point in our evolutionary history, they entered the eukaryotic cell and maintained a symbiotic relationship with the cell, with both the cell and organelle benefiting from the relationship. The fact that they both have their own DNA, RNA, ribosomes, and are capable of reproduction helps to confirm this theory.

Found in plant cells only, the cell wall is composed of cellulose and fibers. It is thick enough for support and protection, yet porous enough to allow water and dissolved substances to enter. Vacuoles are found mostly in plant cells. They hold stored food and pigments. Their large size allows them to fill with water in order to provide turgor pressure. Lack of turgor pressure causes a plant to wilt.

The cytoskeleton, found in both animal and plant cells, is composed of protein filaments attached to the plasma membrane and organelles. They provide a framework for the cell and aid in cell movement. They constantly change shape and move about. Three types of fibers make up the cytoskeleton:

1. Microtubules – the largest of the three, they make up cilia and flagella for locomotion. Some examples are sperm cells, cilia that line the fallopian tubes and tracheal cilia. Centrioles are also composed of microtubules. They aid in cell division to form the spindle fibers that pull the cell apart into two new cells. Centrioles are not found in the cells of higher plants.

2. Intermediate filaments – intermediate in size, they are smaller than microtubules but larger than microfilaments. They help the cell to keep its shape.

3. Microfilaments – smallest of the three, they are made of actin and small amounts of myosin (like in muscle tissue). They function in cell movement like cytoplasmic streaming, endocytosis, and ameboid movement. This structure pinches the two cells apart after cell division, forming two new cells.

The following is a diagram of a generalized animal cell.

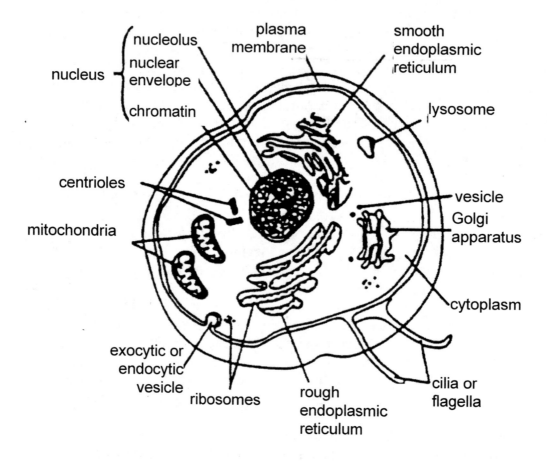

Skill 6.4   **Relating the structures of specialized cells to their functions (e.g., red blood cells, guard cells, neurons)**

All living organisms are composed of cells. Multicellular organisms such as animals and plants are made up of millions of cells that collectively perform the complex biological functions necessary for survival. Multicellular organisms demonstrate a higher level of cell organization where most cells are organized into groups of like cells called tissues. Tissues are assemblages of specialized cells designated to carry out specific functions. Such specialized cells often demonstrate individuated structures that reflect the particular function these cells are required to perform.

Red blood cells (RBCs or erythrocytes) are specialized cells responsible for transporting oxygen from the lungs or gills to the body tissue via the blood. In mammals, these cells have no cell nucleus and lack many standard organelles, such as mitochondria. These cells instead produce energy by fermentation. The lack of most common cellular organelles allows for the characteristic flat, dislike shape and depressed center of mammalian red blood cells. This shape maximizes surface area of RBCs, which in turn increases oxygen diffusion capabilities. The shape of RBCs also allows for a high degree of flexibility, enabling these cells to move through the smallest of capillaries.

Nerve cells (neurons) are another type of highly specialized cell. The physical structure of neurons reflects their function: to rapidly respond to and to transmit stimuli. These extremely long cells consist of a cell body containing ribosomes and mitochondria. From the cell body branch extensions known as dendrites that are responsible for receiving messages and conducting impulses toward the cell body. The axon is the main extension of the neuron that ends in terminal branching fibers where impulses are converted to chemical messages. This part of the neuron carries impulses from the cell body toward other neurons, muscles or glands. The axon is encased in a layer of fatty cells known as the Myelin Sheath. The Myelin Sheath insulation, lengthy axon and input and output extensions all work together to rapidly and effectively transmit neutral impulses.

Muscle cells are another type of specialized cells. Muscle cells are capable of contraction and relaxation, enabling them to control the movement of the body. Individual muscle cells, known as a muscle fibers or myocytes, are organized into bundles to make up three different types of muscle tissue: skeletal muscle, smooth muscle, and cardiac muscle. Because muscle cells must generate large amounts of force, these cells contain myofibrils, the contractile unit of muscles, as well as enlarged mitochondria to produce more energy. Skeletal muscle is the type of striated tissue attached to the skeleton. In mammals, skeletal muscle cells are elongated and multinucleated, and nuclei are located on the periphery of the cell. Such an arrangement allows for more myofibrils in the central part of the cell, allowing for stronger and more efficient muscle movement. A

COMPETENCY 7.0   **UNDERSTAND THE BASIC CHEMICAL COMPONENTS AND REACTIONS OF CELLS.**

Skill 7.1   **Identifying the basic chemical structures of carbohydrates, lipids, proteins, and nucleic acids, the interactions among these compounds, their roles in cells, and their roles in living systems**

Chemical bonds are formed when atoms with incomplete valence shells share or completely transfer their valence electrons. There are three types of chemical bonds, covalent and ionic bonds being stronger than hydrogen bonds.

Covalent bonding is the sharing of a pair of valence electrons by two atoms. A simple example of this is two hydrogen atoms. Each hydrogen atom has one valence electron in its outer shell, therefore the two hydrogen atoms come together to share their electrons. Some atoms share two pairs of valence electrons, like two oxygen atoms. This is called a double covalent bond.

The attraction for the electrons of a covalent bond is called electronegativity. The stronger the electronegativity of an atom, the more it pulls the shared electrons towards itself. Electronegativity defines whether atoms are in a polar or nonpolar covalent bond. In nonpolar covalent bonds, the electrons are shared equally, thus the electronegativity of the two atoms is the same. This type of bonding usually occurs between two of the same atoms. A polar covalent bond is mostly formed when different atoms join, as in hydrogen and oxygen to create water. In this case, oxygen is more electronegative than hydrogen so the oxygen pulls the hydrogen electrons toward itself.

Ionic bonds are formed when one electron is stripped away from its atom to join another atom. In example of this is sodium chloride (NaCl). A single electron on the outer shell of sodium joins the chloride atom with seven electrons in its outer shell. The sodium now has a +1 charge and the chloride now has a -1 charge. The charges attract each other to form an ionic bond. Ionic compounds are called salts. In a dry salt crystal, the bond is so strong it requires a great deal of strength to break it apart. But, place the salt crystal in water, and the bond dissolves easily as the attraction between the two atoms decreases.

The weakest of the three bonds is the hydrogen bond. A hydrogen bond is formed when one electronegative atom shares a hydrogen atom with another electronegative atom. An example of a hydrogen bond is water (H_2O) bonding with ammonia (NH_3). The H^+ attracts the negatively charged nitrogen in a weak bond. Weak hydrogen bonds are beneficial because they can briefly form, the atoms can respond to one another, and then break apart to bond to another. This is a very important role in the chemistry of life.

A compound consists of two or more elements. There are four major chemical compounds found in the cells and bodies of living things. These include carbohydrates, lipids, proteins and nucleic acids.

Monomers are the simplest unit of structure. Monomers can be combined to form polymers, or long chains, making a large variety of molecules possible. Monomers combine through the process of condensation reaction (also called dehydration synthesis). In this process, one molecule of water is removed between each of the adjoining molecules. In order to break the molecules apart in a polymer, water molecules are added between monomers, thus breaking the bonds between them. This is called hydrolysis.

Carbohydrates contain a ratio of two hydrogen atoms for each carbon and oxygen $(CH_2O)_n$. Carbohydrates include sugars and starches. They function in the release of energy. Monosaccharides are the simplest sugars and include glucose, fructose, and galactose. They are major nutrients for cells. In cellular respiration, the cells extract the energy in glucose molecules. Disaccharides are made by joining two monosaccharides by condensation to form a glycosidic linkage (covalent bond between two monosaccharides). Maltose is formed from the combination of two glucose molecules, lactose is formed from joining glucose and galactose, and sucrose is formed from the combination of glucose and fructose. Polysaccharides consist of many monomers joined. They are storage material hydrolyzed as needed to provide sugar for cells or building material for structures protecting the cell. Examples of polysaccharides include starch, glycogen, cellulose and chitin.

Starch - major energy storage molecule in plants. It is a polymer consisting of glucose monomers.
Glycogen - major energy storage molecule in animals. It is made up of many glucose molecules.
Cellulose - found in plant cell walls, its function is structural. Many animals lack the enzymes necessary to hydrolyze cellulose, so it simply adds bulk (fiber) to the diet.
Chitin - found in the exoskeleton of arthropods and fungi. Chitin contains an amino sugar (glycoprotein).

Lipids are composed of glycerol (an alcohol) and three fatty acids. Lipids are hydrophobic (water fearing) and will not mix with water. There are three important families of lipids, fats, phospholipids and steroids.

Fats consist of glycerol (alcohol) and three fatty acids. Fatty acids are long carbon skeletons. The nonpolar carbon-hydrogen bonds in the tails of fatty acids are why they are hydrophobic. Fats are solids at room temperature and come from animal sources (butter, lard).

Phospholipids are a vital component in cell membranes. In a phospholipid, one or two fatty acids are replaced by a phosphate group linked to a nitrogen group. They consist of a polar (charged) head that is hydrophilic or water loving and a nonpolar (uncharged) tail which is hydrophobic or water fearing. This allows the membrane to orient itself with the polar heads facing the interstitial fluid found outside the cell and the internal fluid of the cell.

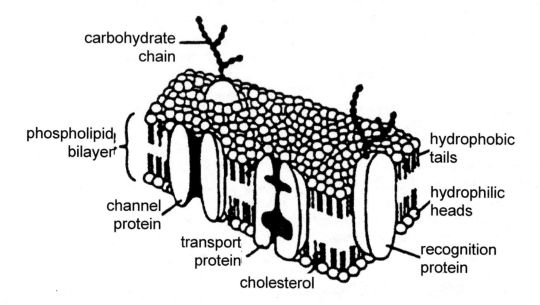

Steroids are insoluble and are composed of a carbon skeleton consisting of four inter-connected rings. An important steroid is cholesterol, which is the precursor from which other steroids are synthesized. Hormones, including cortisone, testosterone, estrogen, and progesterone, are steroids. Their insolubility keeps them from dissolving in body fluids.

Proteins compose about fifty percent of the dry weight of animals and bacteria. Proteins function in structure and aid in support (connective tissue, hair, feathers, quills), storage of amino acids (albumin in eggs, casein in milk), transport of substances (hemoglobin), hormonal to coordinate body activities (insulin), membrane receptor proteins, contraction (muscles, cilia, flagella), body defense (antibodies), and as enzymes to speed up chemical reactions.

All proteins are made of twenty amino acids. An amino acid contains an amino group and an acid group. The radical group varies and defines the amino acid. Amino acids form through condensation reactions with the removal of water. The bond that is formed between two amino acids is called a peptide bond. Polymers of amino acids are called polypeptide chains. An analogy can be drawn between the twenty amino acids and the alphabet. Millions of words can be formed using an alphabet of only twenty-six letters. This diversity is also possible using only twenty amino acids. This results in the formation of many different proteins, whose structure defines the function.

There are four levels of protein structure: primary, secondary, tertiary, and quaternary.

Primary structure is the protein's unique sequence of amino acids. A slight change in primary structure can affect a protein's conformation and its ability to function. Secondary structure is the coils and folds of polypeptide chains. The coils and folds are the result of hydrogen bonds along the polypeptide backbone. The secondary structure is either in the form of an alpha helix or a pleated sheet. The alpha helix is a coil held together by hydrogen bonds. A pleated sheet is the polypeptide chain folding back and forth. The hydrogen bonds between parallel regions hold it together. Tertiary structure is formed by bonding between the side chains of the amino acids. Disulfide bridges are created when two sulfhydryl groups on the amino acids bond together to form a strong covalent bond. Quaternary structure is the overall structure of the protein from the aggregation of two or more polypeptide chains. An example of this is hemoglobin. Hemoglobin consists of two kinds of polypeptide chains.

Nucleic acids consist of DNA (deoxyribonucleic acid) and RNA (ribonucleic acid). Nucleic acids contain the instructions for the amino acid sequence of proteins and the instructions for replicating. The monomer of nucleic acids is called a nucleotide. A nucleotide consists of a 5 carbon sugar, (deoxyribose in DNA, ribose in RNA), a phosphate group, and a nitrogenous base. The base sequence codes for the instructions. There are five bases: adenine, thymine, cytosine, guanine, and uracil. Uracil is found only in RNA and replaces the thymine. A summary of nucleic acid structure can be seen in the table below:

	SUGAR	PHOSPHATE	BASES
DNA	deoxy-ribose	present	adenine, thymine, cytosine, guanine
RNA	ribose	present	adenine, uracil, cytosine, guanine

Due to the molecular structure, adenine will always pair with thymine in DNA or uracil in RNA. Cytosine always pairs with guanine in both DNA and RNA. This allows for the symmetry of the DNA molecule seen below.

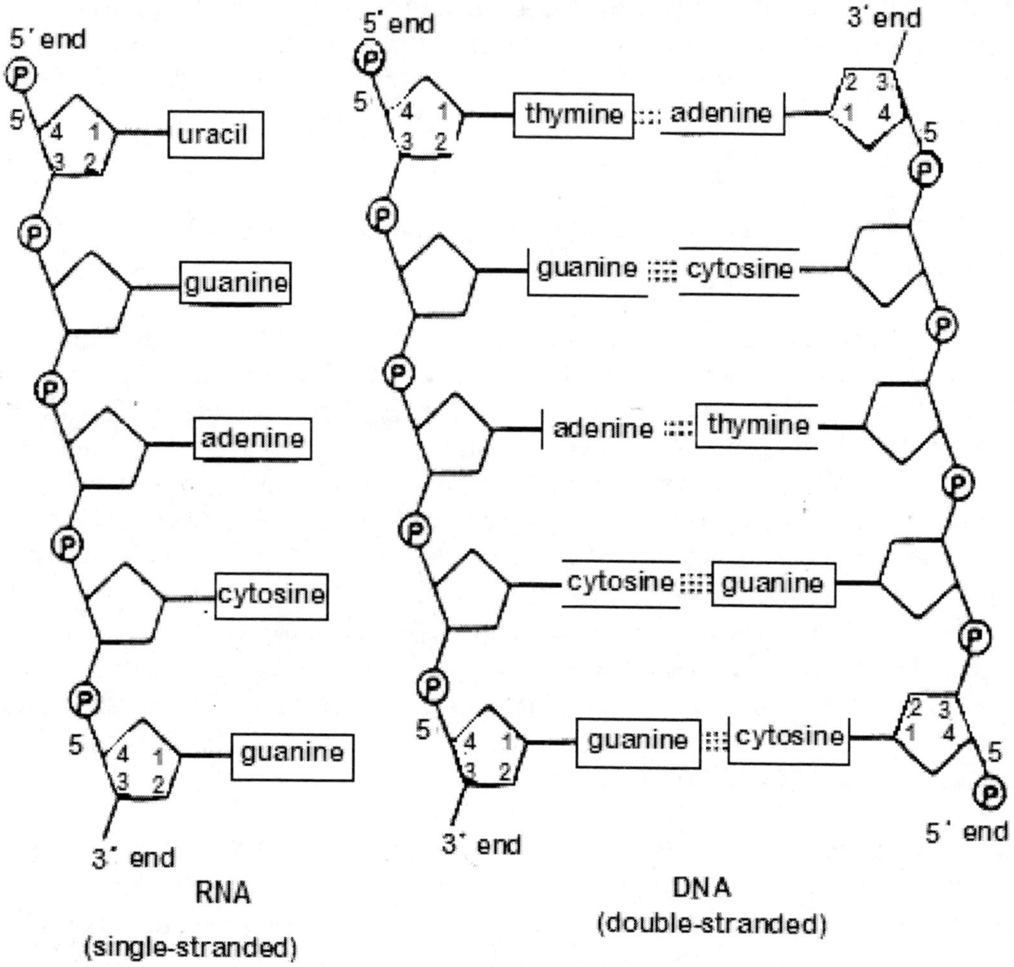

RNA

(single-stranded)

DNA
(double-stranded)

Adenine and thymine (or uracil) are linked by two covalent bonds and cytosine and guanine are linked by three covalent bonds. The guanine and cytosine bonds are harder to break apart than thymine (uracil) and adenine because of the greater number of these bonds. The DNA molecule is called a double helix due to its twisted ladder shape.

Skill 7.2   Demonstrating knowledge of the reactions by which biological macromolecules are metabolized

Metabolism is the sum of all the chemical changes in a cell that convert nutrients to energy and macromolecules, the complex chemical molecules important to cell structure and function. The four main classes of macromolecules are polysaccharides (carbohydrates), nucleic acids, proteins, and lipids. Metabolism consists of two contrasting processes, anabolism and catabolism. Anabolism is biosynthesis, the formation of complex macromolecules from simple precursors. Anabolic reactions require the input of energy to proceed. Catabolism is the breaking down of macromolecules obtained from the environment or cellular reserves to produce energy in the form of ATP and basic precursor molecules. The energy produced by catabolic reactions drives the anabolic pathways of the cell.

Anabolism

The anabolic pathways of a cell diverge, synthesizing a large variety of macromolecules. All anabolic reactions produce complex molecules by linking small subunits, called monomers, together to form a large unit, or polymer. The main mechanism of anabolism is condensation reactions that covalently link monomer units and release water.

Polysaccharides (carbohydrates) consist of monosaccharide units (e.g. glucose) linked together by glycosidic linkages, covalent bonds formed through condensation reactions. Glycogen is the principle storage form of glucose in animal and human cells. Cells produce glycogen by linking glucose monomers to form polymer chains.

Nucleic acids are large polymers of nucleotides. Cells link nucleotides, consisting of a five-carbon sugar, a phosphate group, and a nitrogenous base, through condensation reactions. During DNA and RNA synthesis, the template molecule dictates the sequence of nucleotides by complementary base pairing.

Proteins are large polymers of amino acid subunits called polypeptides. Cells synthesize proteins by linking amino acids, forming peptide linkages through condensation reactions. RNA sequences direct the synthesis of proteins.

Lipids are a diverse group of molecules that are hydrophobic, insoluble in water. Cells synthesize lipids from fatty acid chains formed by the addition of two-carbon units derived from a molecule called acetyl coenzyme A (acetyl-CoA). The reactions involved in lipid synthesis include condensation, oxidation/reduction, and alkylation.

Catabolism

The catabolic pathways of a cell break down macromolecules and produce energy to drive the anabolic pathways. In addition, catabolic pathways release precursor molecules (e.g. amino acids, nucleotides) used in biosynthesis. The basic reaction of catabolism is hydrolysis, the addition of a water molecule across a covalent bond.

Cells break the glycosidic linkages of stored or consumed polysaccharides, releasing glucose or other sugars that can be converted to glucose. The cells further degrade glucose to basic chemical end products, producing energy in the form of ATP.

Cells break down consumed proteins into amino acid units and other simple derivatives. Cells then use the amino acids to form new peptide chains or convert the derivative units into new amino acids. Cells can also acquire energy from the degradation of proteins, but the energy yield is not as high as that of polysaccharides and fatty acids.

Hydrolysis of lipids releases fatty acids that are a rich energy source. Fatty acids contain more than twice as much potential energy as do carbohydrates or proteins. The break down of fatty acids produces basic chemical compounds and energy in the form of ATP.

Finally, hydrolysis of nucleic acids by enzymes produces oligonucleotides (short strings of DNA or RNA) that are further degraded to produce free nucleosides (sugar-nitrogenous base units). Cells further digest nucleosides, separating the nitrogenous base from the sugar. Digestion of nucleosides ultimately results in the production of nitrogenous bases, simple sugars, and basic precursor compounds used in the synthesis of new DNA or RNA.

Skill 7.3   Recognizing the physical and chemical properties of water and its role in living organisms

Water is necessary for life. Its properties are due to its molecular structure and it is an important solvent in biological compounds. Water is a polar substance. This means it is formed by covalent bonds that make it electrically lopsided.

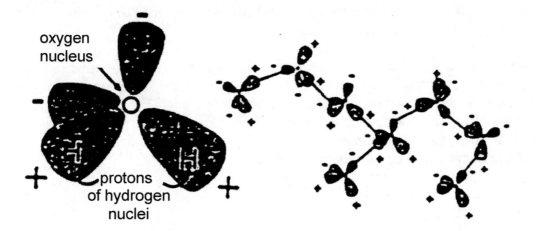

A water molecule showing polarity created by covalent bonds.

Hydrogen bonding between water molecules.

Water molecules are attracted to other water molecules due to this electrical attraction and allows for two important properties: adhesion and cohesion.

Adhesion is when water sticks to other substances like the xylem of a stem which aids the water in traveling up the stem to the leaves.

Cohesion is the ability of water molecules to stick to each other by hydrogen bonds. This allows for surface tension on a body of water or capillarity which allows water to move through vessels. Surface tension is how difficult it is to stretch or break the surface of a liquid. Cohesion allows water to move against gravity.

There are several other important properties of water. Water is a good solvent. An aqueous solution is one in which water is the solvent. It provides a medium for chemical reactions to occur. Water has a high specific heat of 1 calorie per gram per degree Celsius, allowing it to cool and warm slowly, allowing organisms to adapt to temperature changes. Water has a high boiling point it is a good coolant. Its ability to evaporate stabilizes the environment and allows organisms to maintain body temperature. Water has a high freezing point and a lower density as a solid than as a liquid. Water is most dense at four degrees centigrade. This allows ice to float on top of water so a whole body of water does not freeze during the winter. In this way, animals may survive the winter.

Skill 7.4   Analyzing the structure and function of enzymes and factors that affect enzyme function

Enzymes act as biological catalysts to speed up reactions. Enzymes are the most diverse of all types of proteins. They are not used up in a reaction and are recyclable. Each enzyme is specific for a single reaction. Enzymes act on a substrate. The substrate is the material to be broken down or put back together. Most enzymes end in the suffix -ase (lipase, amylase). The prefix is the substrate being acted on (lipids, sugars).

$$\text{Substrate} \xrightarrow{\text{Enzyme}} \text{Product}$$

The active site is the region of the enzyme that binds to the substrate. There are two theories for how the active site functions. The lock and key theory states that the shape of the enzyme is specific because it fits into the substrate like a key fits into a lock. It aids in holding molecules close together so reactions can easily occur.
The Induced fit theory states that an enzyme can stretch and bend to fit the substrate. This is the most accepted theory.

Many factors can affect enzyme activity. Temperature and pH are two of those factors. The temperature can affect the rate of reaction of an enzyme. The optimal pH for enzymes is between 6 and 8, with a few enzymes whose optimal pH falls out of this range.

Cofactors aid in the enzyme's function. Cofactors may be inorganic or organic. Organic cofactors are known as coenzymes. An example of a coenzyme is vitamins. Some chemicals can inhibit an enzymes function. Competitive inhibitors block the substrate from entering the active site of the enzyme to reduce productivity. Noncompetitive inhibitors bind to the enzyme in a location not in the active site but still interrupt substrate binding. In most cases, noncompetitive inhibitors alter the shape of the enzyme. An allosteric enzyme can exist in two shapes; they are active in one form and inactive in the other. Overactive enzymes may cause metabolic diseases.

COMPETENCY 8.0 ANALYZE THE PHYSIOLOGICAL PROCESSES OF CELLS.

Skill 8.1 **Applying knowledge of the biochemical pathways used to synthesize and break down macromolecules, including photosynthesis and respiration, and comparing the transformations of energy and flow of matter during photosynthesis and respiration**

Cellular respiration is the metabolic pathway in which food (glucose, etc.) is broken down to produce energy in the form of ATP. Both plants and animals utilize respiration to create energy for metabolism. In respiration, energy is released by the transfer of electrons in a process know as an oxidation-reduction (redox) reaction. The oxidation phase of this reaction is the loss of an electron and the reduction phase is the gain of an electron. Redox reactions are important for the stages of respiration.

Glycolysis is the first step in respiration. It occurs in the cytoplasm of the cell and does not require oxygen. Each of the ten stages of glycolysis is catalyzed by a specific enzyme. The following is a summary of those stages.

In the first stage the reactant is glucose. For energy to be released from glucose, it must be converted to a reactive compound. This conversion occurs through the phosphorylation of a molecule of glucose by the use of two molecules of ATP. This is an investment of energy by the cell. The six carbon product, called fructose -1,6- bisphosphate, breaks into two 3-carbon molecules of sugar. A phosphate group is added to each sugar molecule and hydrogen atoms are removed. Hydrogen is picked up by NAD^+ (a vitamin). Since there are two sugar molecules, two molecules of NADH are formed. The reduction (adding of hydrogen) of NAD allows the potential of energy transfer. As the phosphate bonds are broken, ATP is made. Two ATP molecules are generated as each original 3 carbon sugar molecule is converted to pyruvic acid (pyruvate). A total of four ATP molecules are made in the four stages. Since two molecules of ATP were needed to start the reaction in stage 1, there is a net gain of two ATP molecules at the end of glycolysis. This accounts for only two percent of the total energy in a molecule of glucose.

Beginning with pyruvate, which was the end product of glycolysis, the following steps occur before entering the Krebs cycle.

1. Pyruvic acid is changed to acetyl-CoA (coenzyme A). This is a three carbon pyruvic acid molecule which has lost one molecule of carbon dioxide (CO_2) to become a two carbon acetyl group. Pyruvic acid loses a hydrogen to NAD^+ which is reduced to NADH.

2.   Acetyl CoA enters the Krebs cycle. For each molecule of glucose it started with, two molecules of Acetyl CoA enter the Krebs cycle (one for each molecule of pyruvic acid formed in glycolysis).

The Krebs cycle (also known as the citric acid cycle), occurs in four major steps. First, the two-carbon acetyl CoA combines with a four-carbon molecule to form a six-carbon molecule of citric acid. Next, two carbons are lost as carbon dioxide (CO_2) and a four-carbon molecule is formed to become available to join with CoA to form citric acid again. Since we started with two molecules of CoA, two turns of the Krebs cycle are necessary to process the original molecule of glucose. In the third step, eight hydrogen atoms are released and picked up by FAD and NAD (vitamins and electron carriers).

Lastly, for each molecule of CoA (remember there were two to start with) you get:

> 3 molecules of NADH x 2 cycles
> 1 molecule of $FADH_2$ x 2 cycles
> 1 molecule of ATP x 2 cycles

Therefore, this completes the breakdown of glucose. At this point, a total of four molecules of ATP have been made; two from glycolysis and one from each of the two turns of the Krebs cycle. Six molecules of carbon dioxide have been released; two prior to entering the Krebs cycle, and two for each of the two turns of the Krebs cycle. Twelve carrier molecules have been made; ten NADH and two $FADH_2$. These carrier molecules will carry electrons to the electron transport chain. ATP is made by substrate level phosphorylation in the Krebs cycle. Notice that the Krebs cycle in itself does not produce much ATP, but functions mostly in the transfer of electrons to be used in the electron transport chain where the most ATP is made.

In the Electron Transport Chain, NADH transfers electrons from glycolysis and the Kreb's cycle to the first molecule in the chain of molecules embedded in the inner membrane of the mitochondrion. Most of the molecules in the electron transport chain are proteins. Nonprotein molecules are also part of the chain and are essential for the catalytic functions of certain enzymes. The electron transport chain does not make ATP directly. Instead, it breaks up a large free energy drop into a more manageable amount. The chain uses electrons to pump H^+ across the mitochondrion membrane. The H^+ gradient is used to form ATP synthesis in a process called chemiosmosis (oxidative phosphorylation). ATP synthetase and energy generated by the movement of hydrogen ions coming off of NADH and $FADH_2$ builds ATP from ADP on the inner membrane of the mitochondria. Each NADH yields three molecules of ATP (10 x 3) and each $FADH_2$ yields two molecules of ATP (2 x 2). Thus, the electron transport chain and oxidative phosphorylation produces 34 ATP.

So, the net gain from the whole process of respiration is 36 molecules of ATP:

> Glycolysis - 4 ATP made, 2 ATP spent = net gain of 2 ATP
> Acetyl CoA- 2 ATP used
> Krebs cycle - 1 ATP made for each turn of the cycle = net gain of 2 ATP
> Electron transport chain - 34 ATP gained

Glycolysis generates ATP with oxygen (aerobic) or without oxygen (anaerobic). Aerobic respiration has already been discussed. Anaerobic respiration can occur by fermentation. ATP can be generated by fermentation by substrate level phosphorylation if there is enough NAD^+ present to accept electrons during oxidation. In anaerobic respiration, NAD^+ is regenerated by transferring electrons to pyruvate. There are two common types of fermentation.

In alcoholic fermentation, pyruvate is converted to ethanol in two steps. In the first step, carbon dioxide is released from the pyruvate. In the second step, ethanol is produced by the reduction of acetaldehyde by NADH. This results in the regeneration of NAD^+ for glycolysis. Alcohol fermentation is carried out by yeast and some bacteria.

Pyruvate is reduced to form lactate as a waste product by NADH in the process of lactic acid fermentation. Animal cells and some bacteria that do not use oxygen utilize lactic acid fermentation to make ATP. Lactic acid forms when pyruvic acid accepts hydrogen from NADH. A buildup of lactic acid is what causes muscle soreness following exercise.

Energy remains stored in the lactic acid or alcohol until needed. This is not an efficient type of respiration. When oxygen is present, aerobic respiration occurs after glycolysis.

Both aerobic and anaerobic pathways oxidize glucose to pyruvate by glycolysis and both pathways have NAD^+ as the oxidizing agent. A substantial difference between the two pathways is that in fermentation, an organic molecule such as pyruvate or acetaldehyde is the final electron acceptor. In respiration, the final electron acceptor is oxygen. Another key difference is that respiration yields much more energy from a sugar molecule than fermentation does. Respiration can produce up to 18 times more ATP than fermentation.

Photosynthesis is an anabolic process that stores energy in the form of a three carbon sugar. We will use glucose as an example for this section. Photosynthesis is done only by organisms that contain chloroplasts (plants, some bacteria, some protists). There are a few terms to be familiar with when discussing photosynthesis.

An autotroph (self feeder) is an organism that make its own food from the energy of the sun or other elements. Autotrophs include phototrophs and chemotrophs.

photoautotrophs - make food from light and carbon dioxide releasing oxygen that can be used for respiration.

chemoautotrophs - oxidize sulfur and ammonia; this is done by some bacteria.

Heterotrophs (other feeder) are organisms that must eat other living things for their energy. Consumers are the same as heterotroph; all animals are heterotrophs. Decomposers break down once living things. Bacteria and fungi are examples of decomposers. Scavengers eat dead things. Examples of scavengers are bacteria, fungi and some animals.

The chloroplast is the site of photosynthesis. It is similar to the mitochondria due to the increased surface area of the thylakoid membrane. It also contains a fluid called stroma between the stacks of thylakoids. The thylakoid membrane contains pigments (chlorophyll) that are capable of capturing light energy.

Photosynthesis reverses the electron flow. Water is split by the chloroplast into hydrogen and oxygen. The oxygen is given off as a waste product as carbon dioxide is reduced to sugar (glucose). This requires the input of energy, which comes from the sun.

Photosynthesis occurs in two stages: the light reactions and the Calvin cycle (dark reactions). The conversion of solar energy to chemical energy occurs in the light reactions. Electrons are transferred by the absorption of light by chlorophyll and cause the water to split, releasing oxygen as a waste product. The chemical energy that is created in the light reaction is in the form of NADPH. ATP is also produced by a process called photophosphorylation. These forms of energy are produced in the thylakoids and are used in the Calvin cycle to produce sugar.

The second stage of photosynthesis is the Calvin cycle. Carbon dioxide in the air is incorporated into organic molecules already in the chloroplast. The NADPH produced in the light reaction is used as reducing power for the reduction of the carbon to carbohydrate. ATP from the light reaction is also needed to convert carbon dioxide to carbohydrate (sugar).

The process of photosynthesis is made possible by the presence of the sun. Visible light ranges in wavelengths of 750 nanometers (red light) to 380 nanometers (violet light). As wavelength decreases, the amount of energy available increases. Light is carried as photons, which is a fixed quantity of energy. Light is reflected (what we see), transmitted, or absorbed (what the plant uses). The plant's pigments capture light of specific wavelengths. Remember that the light that is reflected is what we see as color. Plant pigments include:

Chlorophyll *a* - reflects green/blue light; absorbs red light
Chlorophyll *b* - reflects yellow/green light; absorbs red light
Carotenoids - reflects yellow/orange; absorbs violet/blue

The pigments absorb photons. The energy from the light excites electrons in the chlorophyll that jump to orbitals with more potential energy and reach an "excited" or unstable state.

The formula for photosynthesis is:

$$CO_2 + H_2O + \text{energy (from sunlight)} \rightarrow C_6H_{12}O_6 + O_2$$

The high energy electrons are trapped by primary electron acceptors which are located on the thylakoid membrane. These electron acceptors and the pigments form reaction centers called photosystems that are capable of capturing light energy. Photosystems contain a reaction-center chlorophyll that releases an electron to the primary electron acceptor. This transfer is the first step of the light reactions. There are two photosystems, named according to their date of discovery, not their order of occurrence.

Photosystem I is composed of a pair of chlorophyll *a* molecules. Photosystem I is also called P700 because it absorbs light of 700 nanometers. Photosystem I makes ATP whose energy is needed to build glucose.

Photosystem II - this is also called P680 because it absorbs light of 680 nanometers. Photosystem II produces ATP + $NADPH_2$ and the waste gas oxygen.

Both photosystems are bound to the thylakoid membrane, close to the electron acceptors.

The production of ATP is termed photophosphorylation due to the use of light. Photosystem I uses cyclic photophosphorylation because the pathway occurs in a cycle. It can also use noncyclic photophosphorylation which starts with light and ends with glucose. Photosystem II uses noncyclic photophosphorylation only.

Below is a diagram of the relationship between cellular respiration and photosynthesis.

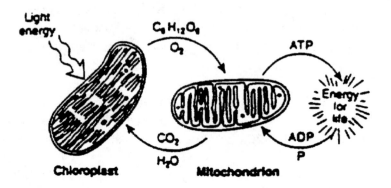

Skill 8.2   Analyzing the roles of active and passive transport processes in cellular homeostasis

In order to understand cellular transport, it is important to know about the structure of the cell membrane. All organisms contain cell membranes because they regulate the flow of materials into and out of the cell. The current model for the cell membrane is the Fluid Mosaic Model because of the ability of lipids and proteins to move and change places, giving the membrane fluidity.

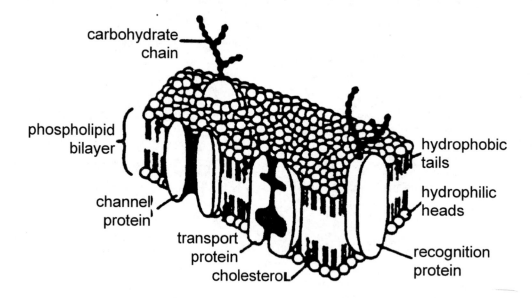

Cell membranes have the following characteristics:

1.   They are made of phospholipids which have polar, charged heads with a phosphate group which is hydrophilic (water loving) and two nonpolar lipid tails which are hydrophobic (water fearing). This allows the membrane to orient itself with the polar heads facing the fluid inside and outside the cell and the hydrophobic lipid tails sandwiched in between. Each individual phospholipid is called a micelle.

2.   They contain proteins embedded inside (integral proteins) and proteins on the surface (peripheral proteins). These proteins may act as channels for transport, may contain enzymes, may act as receptor sites, may act to stick cells together or may attach to the cytoskeleton to give the cell shape.

3.   They contain cholesterol, which alters the fluidity of the membrane.

4.   They contain oligosaccharides (small carbohydrate polymers) on the outside of the membrane. These act as markers that help distinguish one cell from another.

5.   They contain receptors made of glycoproteins that can attach to certain molecules, like hormones. Cell transport is necessary to maintain homeostasis, or balance of the cell with its external environment. Cell membranes are selectively permeable, which is the key to transport. Not all molecules may pass through easily. Some molecules require energy or carrier molecules and may only cross when needed.

Passive transport does not require energy and moves the material with the concentration gradient (high to low). Small molecules may pass through the membrane in this manner. Two examples of passive transport include diffusion and osmosis. Diffusion is the ability of molecules to move from areas of high concentration to areas of low concentration. It normally involves small uncharged particles like oxygen. Osmosis is simply the diffusion of water across a semi-permeable membrane. Osmosis may cause cells to swell or shrink, depending on the internal and external environments. The following terms are used in relation of the cell to the environment.

Isotonic - water concentration is equal inside and outside the cell. Net movement in either direction is basically equal.

Hypertonic - "hyper" refers to the amount of dissolved particles. The more particles in a solution, the lower its water concentration. Therefore, when a cell is hypertonic to its environment, there is more water outside the cell than inside. Water will move into the cell and the cell will swell. If the environment is hypertonic to the cell, there is more water inside the cell. Water will move out of the cell and the cell will shrink.

Hypotonic - "hypo" again refers to the amount of dissolved particles. The less particles in a solution, the higher its water concentration. When a cell is hypotonic to its environment, there is more water inside the cell than outside. Water will move out of the cell and the cell will shrink. If the environment is hypotonic to the cell, there is more water outside the cell than inside. Water will move into the cell and the cell will swell.

The facilitated diffusion mechanism does not require energy, but does require a carrier protein. An example would be insulin, which is needed to carry glucose into the cell.

Active transport requires energy. The energy for this process comes from either ATP or an electrical charge difference. Active transport may move materials either with or against a concentration gradient. Some examples of active transport are:

-Calcium pumps - actively pump calcium outside of the cell and are important in nerve and muscle transmission.
-Stomach acid pump - exports hydrogen ions to lower the pH of the stomach and increase acidity.
-Sodium-Potassium pump - maintains an electrical difference across the cell. This is useful in restoring ion balance so nerves can continue to function. It exchanges sodium ions for potassium ions across the plasma membrane in animal cells.

Active transport involves a membrane potential which is a charge on the membrane. The charge works like a magnet and may cause transport proteins to alter their shape, thus allowing substances in or out of the cell.

The transport of large molecules depends on the fluidity of the membrane which is controlled by cholesterol in the membrane. Exocytosis is the release of large particles by the vesicles fusing with the plasma membrane. In the process of endocytosis, the cell takes in macromolecules and particulate matter by forming vesicles derived from the plasma membrane. There are three types of endocytosis in animal cells. Phagocytosis is when a particle is engulfed by pseudopodia and packaged in a vacuole. In pinocytosis, the cell takes in extracellular fluid in small vesicles. Receptor-mediated endocytosis is when the membrane vesicles bud inward to allow a cell to take in large amounts of certain substances. The vesicles have proteins with receptors that are specific for the substance.

COMPETENCY 9.0 **UNDERSTAND THE PROCESSES OF CELL DIVISION, GROWTH, AND DIFFERENTIATION.**

Skill 9.1 **Identifying the stages of the cell cycle, the characteristics of each stage, and the processes, roles, and outcomes of mitosis and meiosis**

Mitosis is divided into two parts: the mitotic (M) phase and interphase. In the mitotic phase, mitosis and cytokinesis divide the nucleus and cytoplasm, respectively. This phase is the shortest phase of the cell cycle. Interphase is the stage where the cell grows and copies the chromosomes in preparation for the mitotic phase. Interphase occurs in three stages of growth: G1 (growth) period is when the cell is growing and metabolizing, the S period (synthesis) is where new DNA is being made and the G2 phase (growth) is where new proteins and organelles are being made to prepare for cell division.

The mitotic phase is a continuum of change, although it is described as occurring in five stages: prophase, prometaphase, metaphase, anaphase, and telophase. During prophase, the cell proceeds through the following steps continuously, with no stopping. The chromatin condenses to become visible chromosomes. The nucleolus disappears and the nuclear membrane breaks apart. Mitotic spindles form that will eventually pull the chromosomes apart. They are composed of microtubules. The cytoskeleton breaks down and the spindles are pushed to the poles or opposite ends of the cell by the action of centrioles. During prometaphase, the nuclear membrane fragments and allows the spindle microtubules to interact with the chromosomes. Kinetochore fibers attach to the chromosomes at the centromere region. (Sometimes prometaphase is grouped with metaphase). When the centrosomes are at opposite ends of the cell, the division is in metaphase. The centromeres of all the chromosomes are aligned with one another. During anaphase, the centromeres split in half and homologous chromosomes separate. The chromosomes are pulled to the poles of the cell, with identical sets at either end. The last stage of mitosis is telophase. Here, two nuclei form with a full set of DNA that is identical to the parent cell. The nucleoli become visible and the nuclear membrane reassembles. A cell plate is seen in plant cells, whereas a cleavage furrow is formed in animal cells. The cell is pinched into two cells. Cytokinesis, or division of the cytoplasm and organelles, occurs.

Below is a diagram of mitosis.

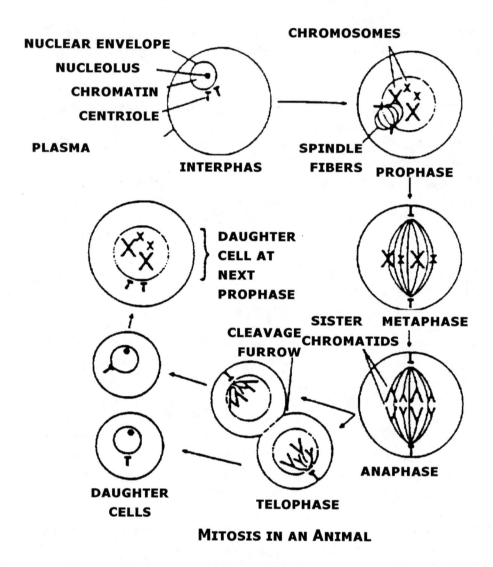

MITOSIS IN AN ANIMAL

Meiosis is similar to mitosis, but there are two consecutive cell divisions, meiosis I and meiosis II in order to reduce the chromosome number by one half. This way, when the sperm and egg join during fertilization, the haploid number is reached.

Similar to mitosis, meiosis is preceded by an interphase during which the chromosome replicates. The steps of meiosis are as follows:

Prophase I – the replicated chromosomes condense and pair with homologues in a process called synapsis. This forms a tetrad. Crossing over, the exchange of genetic material between homologues to further increase diversity, occurs during prophase I.

Metaphase I – the homologous pairs attach to spindle fibers after lining up in the middle of the cell.

Anaphase I – the sister chromatids remain joined and move to the poles of the cell.

Telophase I – the homologous chromosome pairs continue to separate. Each pole now has a haploid chromosome set. Telophase I occurs simultaneously with cytokinesis. In animal cells, cleavage furrows form and cell plate appear in plant cells.

Prophase II – a spindle apparatus forms and the chromosomes condense.

Metaphase II – sister chromatids line up in center of cell. The centromeres divide and the sister chromatids begin to separate.

Anaphase II – the separated chromosomes move to opposite ends of the cell.

Telophase II – cytokinesis occurs, resulting in four haploid daughter cells.

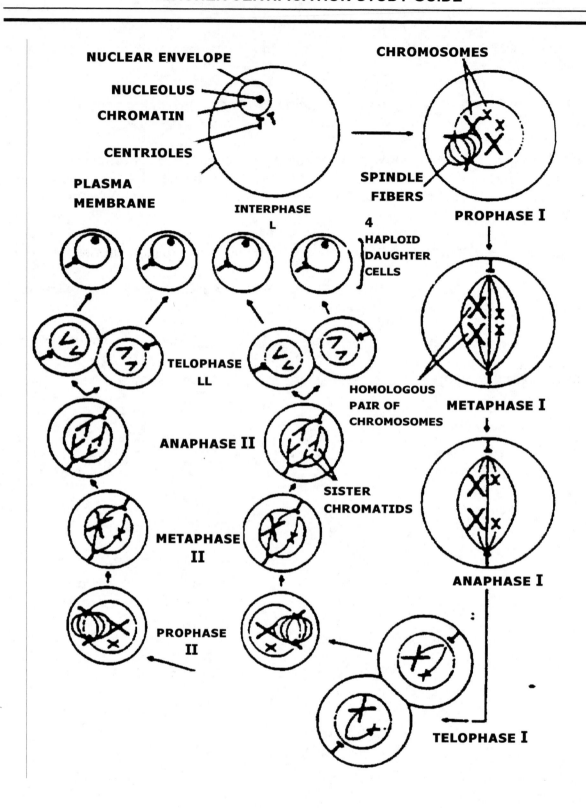

Skill 9.2 Evaluating the roles of cell growth and division in the growth of multicellular organisms

The purpose of cell division is to provide growth and repair in body (somatic) cells and to replenish or create sex cells for reproduction. There are two forms of cell division. Mitosis is the division of somatic cells and meiosis is the division of sex cells (eggs and sperm). Growth and development, as directed by DNA, produces an organism characteristic of its species. In humans and other higher-level mammals, growth and development is a very complex process. In humans, growth and development requires differentiation of cells into many different types to form the various organs, structures, and functional elements. While differentiation is unique to higher level organisms, all living organisms grow. For example, the simplest bacterial cell grows in size until it divides into two organisms. Human body cells undergo a similar process, growing in size until division is necessary.

Skill 9.3 Recognizing characteristics of the process of cell differentiation and its role in development

Differentiation is the process in which cells become specialized in structure and function. The fate of the cell is usually maintained through many subsequent generations. Gene regulatory proteins can generate many cell types during development. Scientists believe that these proteins are passed down to the next generation of cells to ensure the specialized expression of the genes occurs.

Stem cells are not terminally differentiated. It can divide for as long as the animal is alive. When the stem cell divides, its daughter cells can either remain a stem cell or can go forth with terminal differentiation. There are many types of stem cells. They are specialized for different classes of terminally differentiated cells.

Embryonic stem cells give rise to all the tissues and cell types in the body. In culture, these cells have led to the creation of animal tissue that can replace damaged tissues. It is hopeful that with continued research, embryonic stem cells can be cultured to replace muscles, tissues, and organs of individuals whose own are damaged.

Skill 9.4 Analyzing factors that affect cell division, growth, and differentiation

Most cell types respond to both internal and external cues that dictate the processes of cell division, growth, and differentiation. Depending on the type of cell, external cues include environmental factors such as nutrient level and temperature or signaling molecules from surrounding cells. Internal cues refer to the genetic make up of cells (DNA) that directs many of the cell processes, including growth and differentiation.

In prokaryotic cells, environmental conditions direct cell growth. When the environment is favorable – containing ample amounts of nutrients, optimum temperature, and appropriate water levels – cells will grow rapidly. In eukaryotic organisms, cellular DNA and cell-to-cell signaling dictate cell growth. Certain types of cells in multicellular organisms grow more readily than others. In addition, cells release growth factors, small polypeptides, which stimulate growth of surrounding cells.

Cell division occurs when cells become too large to function efficiently. In single-celled organisms, cell division is the method of reproduction when environmental conditions are favorable. In multicellular organisms, cell division replaces worn-out cells. Chemical signaling directs cell division. Most cells can only divide a certain amount of times because telomeres, protective parts of DNA at the end of chromosomes, degrade with each division. Furthermore, some cells, such as nerve cells, generally do not divide once they reach maturity.

Cell differentiation is unique to multicellular organisms. Differentiation is the method by which cells become specialized. DNA often dictates what type the cell will become. In addition, cell signaling plays a key role in differentiation. A special type of cells, pluripotent stem cells, can become any type of adult cell, depending on the chemical signals in the cellular environment.

COMPETENCY 10.0   UNDERSTAND THE CONCEPTS AND PRINCIPLES OF MENDELIAN GENETICS.

Skill 10.1   Evaluating evidence that certain characteristics are inherited

Darwin's theory of natural selection is the basis of all evolutionary theory. His theory has four basic points:

1. Each species produces more offspring than can survive.
2. The individual organisms that make up a larger population are born with certain variations.
3. The overabundance of offspring creates competition for survival among individual organisms (survival of the fittest).
4. Variations are passed down from parent to offspring (inheritance).

Points 2 and 4 form the genetic basis for evolution.

Skill 10.2   Analyzing the significance of Mendel's experiments and their role in formulating the basic principles of heredity (e.g., segregation, independent assortment)

Gregor Mendel is recognized as the father of genetics. His work in the late 1800s is the basis of our knowledge of genetics. Although unaware of the presence of DNA or genes, Mendel realized there were factors (now known as genes) that were transferred from parents to their offspring. Mendel worked with pea plants and fertilized the plants himself, keeping track of subsequent generations which led to the Mendelian laws of genetics. Mendel found that two "factors" governed each trait, one from each parent. Traits or characteristics came in several forms, known as alleles. For example, the trait of flower color had white alleles (pp) and purple alleles (PP). Mendel formed two laws: the law of segregation and the law of independent assortment.

The law of segregation states that only one of the two possible alleles from each parent is passed on to the offspring. If the two alleles differ, then one is fully expressed in the organism's appearance (the dominant allele) and the other has no noticeable effect on appearance (the recessive allele). The two alleles for each trait segregate into different gametes. A Punnet square can be used to show the law of segregation. In a Punnet square, one parent's genes are put at the top of the box and the other parent's on the side. Genes combine in the squares just like numbers are added in addition tables. This Punnet square shows the result of the cross of two F_1 hybrids.

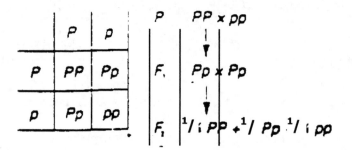

This cross results in a 1:2:1 ratio of F_2 offspring. Here, the P is the dominant allele and the p is the recessive allele. The F_1 cross produces three offspring with the dominant allele expressed (two PP and Pp) and one offspring with the recessive allele expressed (pp). Some other important terms to know:

Homozygous – having a pair of identical alleles. For example, PP and pp are homozygous pairs.

Heterozygous – having two different alleles. For example, Pp is a heterozygous pair.

Phenotype – the organism's physical appearance.

Genotype – the organism's genetic makeup. For example, PP and Pp have the same phenotype (purple in color), but different genotypes.

The law of independent assortment states that alleles sort independently of each other. The law of segregation applies for a monohybrid crosses (only one character, in this case flower color, is experimented with). In a dihybrid cross, two characters are being explored. Two of the seven characters Mendel studied were seed shape and color. Yellow is the dominant seed color (Y) and green is the recessive color (y). The dominant seed shape is round (R) and the recessive shape is wrinkled (r). A cross between a plant with yellow round seeds ($YYRR$) and a plant with green wrinkled seeds ($yyrr$) produces an F_1 generation with the genotype $YyRr$. The production of F_2 offspring results in a 9:3:3:1 phenotypic ratio.

	YR	Yr	yR	yr
YR	YYRR	YYRr	YyRR	YyRr
Yr	YYRr	YYrr	YyRr	Yyrr
yR	YyRR	YyRr	yyRR	yyRr
yr	YyRr	Yyrr	yyRr	yyrr

P   YYRR x yyrr

$\downarrow$

F₁   YyRr

$\downarrow$

F₁

    YYRR - 1 ⎫
    YYRr - 2 ⎪ 9 yellow round
    YyRR - 2 ⎬
    YyRr - 4 ⎭

    yyRR - 1 ⎫ 3 green round
    yyRr - 2 ⎭

    YYrr - 1 ⎫ 3 yellow wrinkled
    Yyrr - 2 ⎭

    yyrr - 1 } 1 green wrinkled

F₂

Skill 10.3   Relating the behavior of chromosomes during meiosis and fertilization to inheritance patterns; recognizing the relationship between genotype and phenotype

Meiosis and fertilization are responsible for genetic diversity. There are several mechanisms that contribute to genetic variation in sexual reproductive organisms. Three of them are independent assortment of chromosomes, crossing over, and random fertilization.

At the metaphase I stage of meiosis, each homologous pair of chromosomes is situated along the metaphase plate. The orientation of the homologous pair is random and independent of the other pairs of metaphase I. This results in an independent assortment of maternal and paternal chromosomes. Based on this information, it seems as though each chromosome in a gamete would be of only maternal or paternal origin. A process called crossing over prevents this from happening.

Crossing over occurs during prophase I. At this point, nonsister chromatids cross and exchange corresponding segments. Crossing over results in the combination of DNA from both parents, allowing for greater genetic variation in sexual life cycles.

Random fertilization gives way to genetic variation. Each parent has about 8 million possible chromosome combinations. This allows for over 60 trillion diploid combinations.

Phenotype is the organism's physical appearance.

Genotype is the organism's genetic makeup. For example, *PP* and *Pp* have the same phenotype (purple in color), but different genotypes.

Skill 10.4 Applying knowledge of dominance, recessiveness, incomplete dominance, and sex linkage to solve problems involving genetic crosses

Based on Mendelian genetics, the more complex hereditary pattern of dominance was discovered. In Mendel's law of segregation, the F_1 generation have either purple or white flowers. This is an example of complete dominance. Incomplete dominance is when the F_1 generation results in an appearance somewhere between the two parents. For example, red flowers are crossed with white flowers, resulting in an F_1 generation with pink flowers. The red and white traits are still carried by the F_1 generation, resulting in an F_2 generation with a phenotypic ration of 1:2:1. In codominance, the genes may form new phenotypes. The ABO blood grouping is an example of codominance. A and B are of equal strength and O is recessive. Therefore, type A blood may have the genotypes of AA or AO, type B blood may have the genotypes of BB or BO, type AB blood has the genotype A and B, and type O blood has two recessive O genes.

A family pedigree is a collection of a family's history for a particular trait. As you work your way through the pedigree of interest, the Mendelian inheritance theories are applied. In tracing a trait, the generations are mapped in a pedigree chart, similar to a family tree but with the alleles present. In a case where both parent have a particular trait and one of two children also express this trait, then the trait is due to a dominant allele. In contrast, if both parents do not express a trait and one of their children do, that trait is due to a recessive allele.

The same techniques of pedigree analysis apply when tracing inherited disorders. Thousands of genetic disorders are the result of inheriting a recessive trait. These disorders range from nonlethal traits (such as albinism) to life-threatening (such as cystic fibrosis).

Most people with recessive disorders are born to parents with normal phenotypes. The mating of heterozygous parents would result in an offspring genotypic ratio of 1:2:1; thus 1 out of 4 offspring would express this recessive trait. The heterozygous parents are called carriers because they do not express the trait phenotypically but pass the trait on to their offspring.

Lethal dominant alleles are much less common than lethal recessives. This is because lethal dominant alleles are not masked in heterozygotes. Mutations in a gene of the sperm or egg can result in a lethal dominant allele, usually killing the developing offspring.

Sex linked traits - the Y chromosome found only in males (XY) carries very little genetic information, whereas the X chromosome found in females (XX) carries very important information. Since men have no second X chromosome to cover up a recessive gene, the recessive trait is expressed more often in men. Women need the recessive gene on both X chromosomes to show the trait. Examples of sex linked traits include hemophilia and color-blindness.

Sex influenced traits - traits are influenced by the sex hormones. Male pattern baldness is an example of a sex influenced trait. Testosterone influences the expression of the gene. Mostly men loose their hair due to this.

Nondisjunction - during meiosis, chromosomes fail to separate properly. One sex cell may get both chromosomes and another may get none. Depending on the chromosomes involved this may or may not be serious. Offspring end up with either an extra chromosome or are missing one. An example of nondisjunction is Down Syndrome, where three #21 chromosomes are present.

Chromosome Theory - Noted by Walter Sutton in the early 1900's. In the late 1800's, the processes of mitosis and meiosis were now understood. Sutton saw how this explanation confirmed Mendel's "factors". The chromosome theory basically states that genes are located on chromosomes. The chromosomes undergo independent assortment and segregation.

Skill 10.5   Analyzing the effects of crossing-over on genotypes and phenotypes

Crossing over occurs during prophase I. At this point, nonsister chromatids cross and exchange corresponding segments. Crossing over results in the combination of DNA from both parents, allowing for greater genetic variation in sexual life cycles.

COMPETENCY 11.0 UNDERSTAND THE CONCEPTS AND PRINCIPLES OF MOLECULAR GENETICS.

Skill 11.1 Identifying the structures and functions of DNA and RNA in organisms

Nucleic acids consist of DNA (deoxyribonucleic acid) and RNA (ribonucleic acid). Nucleic acids contain the instructions for the amino acid sequence of proteins and the instructions for replicating. The monomer of nucleic acids is called a nucleotide. A nucleotide consists of a 5 carbon sugar, (deoxyribose in DNA, ribose in RNA), a phosphate group, and a nitrogenous base. The base sequence codes for the instructions. There are five bases: adenine, thymine, cytosine, guanine, and uracil. Uracil is found only in RNA and replaces the thymine. A summary of nucleic acid structure can be seen in the table below:

	SUGAR	PHOSPHATE	BASES
DNA	deoxy-ribose	present	adenine, thymine, cytosine, guanine
RNA	ribose	present	adenine, uracil, cytosine, guanine

Due to the molecular structure, adenine will always pair with thymine in DNA or uracil in RNA. Cytosine always pairs with guanine in both DNA and RNA. This allows for the symmetry of the DNA molecule seen below.

RNA
(single-stranded)

DNA
(double-stranded)

Adenine and thymine (or uracil) are linked by two covalent bonds and cytosine and guanine are linked by three covalent bonds. The guanine and cytosine bonds are harder to break apart than thymine (uracil) and adenine because of the greater number of these bonds. The DNA molecule is called a double helix due to its twisted ladder shape.

Skill 11.2   Relating the structure of DNA and RNA to the processes of replication, transcription, and translation; analyzing steps in the process of protein synthesis

Replication

DNA replicates semiconservatively. This means the two original strands are conserved and serve as a template for the new strand.

In DNA replication, the first step is to separate the two strands. As they separate, they need to unwind the supercoils to reduce tension. An enzyme called helicase unwinds the DNA as the replication fork proceeds and topoisomerases relieve the tension by nicking one strand and letting the supercoil relax. Once the strands have been separated, they need to be stabilized. Single stranded binding proteins (SSBs) bind to the single strands until the DNA is replicated.

An RNA polymerase called primase adds ribonucleotides to the DNA template to initiate DNA synthesis. This short RNA-DNA hybrid is called a primer. Once the DNA is single stranded, DNA polymerases add nucleotides in the 5' → 3' direction.

As DNA synthesis proceeds along the replication fork, it becomes obvious that replication is semi-discontinuous; meaning one strand is synthesized in the direction the replication fork is moving and the other is synthesizing in the opposite direction. The strand that is continuously synthesized is the leading strand and the discontinuously synthesized strand is the lagging strand. As the replication fork proceeds, new primer is added to the lagging strand and it is synthesized discontinuously in fragments called Okazaki fragments.

The RNA primers that remain need to be removed and replaced with deoxyribonucleotides. DNA polymerase has 5' → 3' polymerase activity and has 3' → 5' exonuclease activity. This enzyme binds to the nick between the Okazaki fragment and the RNA primer. It removes the primer and adds deoxyribonucleotides in the 5' → 3' direction. The nick still remains until DNA ligase seals it with the final product being a double stranded segment of DNA.

Once the double stranded segment is replicated, there is a proofreading system by DNA replication enzymes. In eukaryotes, DNA polymerases have 3' → 5' exonuclease activity—they move backwards and remove nucleotides where the enzyme recognizes an error, then it adds the correct nucleotide in the 5' → 3' direction. In E. coli, DNA polymerase II synthesizes DNA during repair of DNA damage.

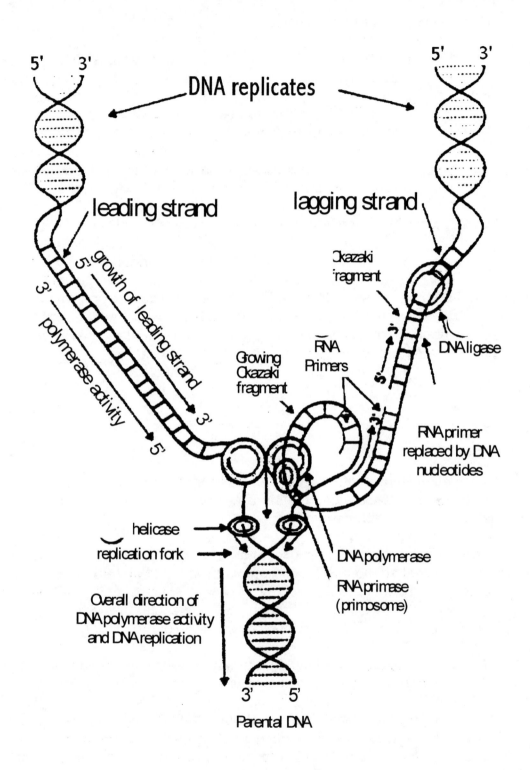

DNA replicates

leading strand

lagging strand

Okazaki fragment

growth of leading strand

polymerase activity

Growing Okazaki fragment

RNA Primers

DNA ligase

RNA primer replaced by DNA nucleotides

helicase

replication fork

DNA polymerase

RNA primase (primosome)

Overall direction of DNA polymerase activity and DNA replication

Parental DNA

Protein synthesis (transcription and translation)

Proteins are synthesized through the processes of transcription and translation. Three major classes of RNA are needed to carry out these processes. The first is messenger RNA (mRNA), which contains information for translation. Ribosomal RNA (rRNA) is a structural component of the ribosome and transfer RNA (tRNA) carries amino acids to the ribosome for protein synthesis.

Transcription is similar in prokaryotes and eukaryotes. During transcription, the DNA molecule is copied into an RNA molecule (mRNA). Transcription occurs through the steps of initiation, elongation, and termination. Transcription also occurs for rRNA and tRNA, but the focus here is on mRNA.

Initiation begins at the promoter of the double stranded DNA molecule. The promoter is a specific region of DNA that directs the RNA polymerase to bind to the DNA. The double stranded DNA opens up and RNA polymerase begins transcription in the 5' → 3' direction by pairing ribonucleotides to the deoxyribonucleotides as follows to get a complementary mRNA segment:

Deoxyribonucleotide		Ribonucleotide
A	→	U
G	→	C

Elongation is the synthesis on the mRNA strand in the 5' → 3' direction. The new mRNA rapidly separates from the DNA template and the complementary DNA strands pair together again.

Termination of transcription occurs at the end of a gene. Cleavage occurs at specific sites on the mRNA. This process is aided by termination factors.

In eukaryotes, mRNA goes through posttranscriptional processing before going on to translation. There are three basic steps of processing:

1.   5' capping is attaching a base with a methyl attached to it that protects 5' end from degradation and serves as the site where ribosome binds to mRNA for translation.
2.   3' polyadenylation is when about 100-300 adenines are added to the free 3' end of mRNA resulting in a poly-A-tail.
3.   Introns (non-coding) are removed and the coding exons are spliced together to form the mature mRNA.

Translation is the process in which the mRNA sequence becomes a polypeptide. The mRNA sequence determines the amino acid sequence of a protein by following a pattern called the genetic code. The genetic code consists of triplet nucleotide combinations called amino acids. There are 20 amino acids mRNA codes for. Amino acids are the building blocks of protein. They are attached together by peptide bonds to form a polypeptide chain. There are 64 triplet combinations called codons. Three codons are termination codons and the remaining 61 code for amino acids.

Ribosomes are the site of translation. They contain rRNA and many proteins. Translation occurs in three steps: initiation, elongation, and termination. Initiation occurs when the methylated tRNA binds to the ribosome to form a complex. This complex then binds to the 5' cap of the mRNA. In elongation, tRNAs carry the amino acid to the ribosome and place it in order according to the mRNA sequence. tRNA is very specific – it only accepts one of the 20 amino acids that corresponds to the anticodon. The anticodon is complementary to the codon. For example, using the codon sequence below:

the mRNA reads A U G / G A G / C A U / G C U
the anticodons are UA C / C U C / G U A / C G A

Termination occurs when the ribosome reaches any one of the stop codons : UAA, UAG, or UGA. The newly formed polypeptide then undergoes posttranslational modification to alter or remove portions of the polypeptide.

Skill 11.3   Recognizing current models of gene structure and function and how gene expression is regulated in various organisms

Gene Structure and Function

Genes are sections of DNA strands that code for the formation of cellular products (e.g. RNA, proteins). DNA is the molecule that encodes genetic information. A DNA molecule is a long, double strand of nitrogenous base pairs linked by hydrogen bonding to form a twisting helix. The four nitrogenous bases found in DNA are adenine (A), thymine (T), guanine (G), and cytosine (C). A specialized protein "reads" the base sequence of genes in units of three and translates the code into amino acids or RNA molecules.

Genes have very complex structures, with many unique regions serving different functions. For example, a typical prokaryotic gene has the following regions:

Recognition region (approximately 50 base pairs in length) – the region of the gene recognized by the RNA polymerase (the protein that transcribes DNA to RNA) for initial binding
Transcription initiation site – the base sequence where the RNA polymerase begins transcription

5' untranslated region – the bases at the starting end of the gene that the cell does not translate into protein or RNA

Translation initiation site – the base sequence that the ribosomes recognize and bind to initiate translation

Coding region – the sequence of bases that determine the function of the gene

Translation stop site – the sequence of bases that instructs the ribosome to stop translation

3' untranslated region – the bases at the end of the gene that the cell does not translate into protein or RNA

Transcription stop site – the base sequence that instructs the RNA polymerase to stop transcription

Eukaryotic genes are similar in structure and are more complex. The main difference between eukaryotic and prokaryotic genes is that the coding region of eukaryotic genes contains both exons (actual coding regions) and introns (non-coding regions).

The central function of genes is to direct the synthesis of cellular material such as protein and RNA. In addition, genes store genetic information allowing organisms to pass genetic traits on to their offspring.

Expression

In bacterial cells, the *lac* operon is a good example of the control of gene expression. The *lac* operon contains the genes that encode for the enzymes used to convert lactose into fuel (glucose and galactose). The *lac* operon contains three genes, *lac Z*, *lac Y*, and *lac A*. *Lac Z* encodes an enzyme for the conversion of lactose into glucose and galactose. *Lac Y* encodes for an enzyme that causes lactose to enter the cell. *Lac A* encodes for an enzyme that acetylates lactose.

The *lac* operon also contains a promoter and an operator that is the "off and on" switch for the operon. A protein called the repressor switches the operon off when it binds to the operator. When lactose is absent, the repressor is active and the operon is turned off. The operon is turned on again when allolactose (formed from lactose) inactivates the repressor by binding to it.

Skill 11.4   Identifying characteristics of the genetic code

Cells read the base sequence of genes three at a time. A three base sequence, called a codon, codes for a specific amino acid that specialized proteins attach to the growing polypeptide chain. Four bases taken three at a time produces 64 possible combinations, more than enough to code for the 20 amino acids. Thus, an amino acid may have from one to six triplet codons that code for it. In addition, three of the codons are stop codons that cause termination of transcription rather than coding for an amino acid.

The genetic code has several important characteristics. First, the code is unambiguous as each codon specifies only one amino acid. Second, the code is redundant as more than one codon may code for a single amino acid. Third, in most cases the third base in a codon plays only a minor role in amino acid recognition and coding. For example, the four codons for alanine all start with GC (GCC, GCA, GCT, and GCG). Fourth, in general codons with similar sequences code for amino acids with similar chemical properties. Finally, the AUG codon that codes for methionine is also a transcription start codon.

It is also important to note that different organisms show different statistical preferences for the use of triplet codons and amino acids. This characteristic is important when attempting to transfer genes between species.

Skill 11.5   Analyzing types of mutations and their consequences

Inheritable changes in DNA are called mutations. Mutations may be errors in replication or a spontaneous rearrangement of one or more segments by factors like radioactivity, drugs, or chemicals. The severity of the change is not as critical as where the change occurs. DNA contains large segments of non-coding areas called introns. The important coding areas are called exons. If an error occurs on an intron, there is no effect. If the error occurs on an exon, it may be minor to lethal depending on the severity of the mistake. Mutations may occur on somatic or sex cells. Usually the mutations on sex cells are more dangerous since they contain the basis of all information for the developing offspring. But mutations are not always bad. They are the basis of evolution and if they make a more favorable variation that enhances the organism's survival, then they are beneficial. But mutations may also lead to abnormalities and birth defects and even death. There are several types of mutations.

A point mutation is a mutation involving a single nucleotide or a few adjacent nucleotides. Let's suppose a normal sequence was as follows:

Normal:	A B C D E F
Duplication - one gene is repeated	A B C C D E F
Inversion - a segment of the sequence is flipped	A E D C B F
Deletion - a gene is left out	A B C E F (D is lost)
Insertion or Translocation - a segment from another place on the DNA is stuck in the wrong place	A B C R S D E F
Breakage - a piece is lost	A B C (DEF is lost)

Deletion and insertion mutations that shift the reading frame are frame shift mutations. A silent mutation makes no change in the amino acid sequence, therefore it does not alter the protein function. A missense mutation results in an alteration in the amino acid sequence.

SCHOOL OF EDUCATION
CURRICULUM LABORATORY
UM-DEARBORN

A mutation's effect on protein function depends on which amino acid is involved and how many are involved. The structure of a protein usually determines its function. A mutation that does not alter the structure will probably have little or no effect on the protein's function. However, a mutation that does alter the structure of a protein can severely affect protein activity is called loss-of-function mutation. Sickle-cell anemia and cystic fibrosis are examples of loss-of-function mutations.

Sickle-cell anemia is characterized by weakness, heart failure, joint and muscular impairment, fatigue, abdominal pain and dysfunction, impaired mental function, and eventual death. The mutation that causes this genetic disorder is a point mutation in the sixth amino acid. A normal hemoglobin molecule has glutamic acid as the sixth amino acid and the sickle-cell hemoglobin has valine at the sixth position. This causes the chemical properties of hemoglobin to change. The hemoglobin of a sickle-cell person has a lower affinity for oxygen, and that causes red blood cells to have a sickle shape. The sickle shape of the red blood cell does not allow the cells to pass through capillaries well, forming clogs.

Cystic fibrosis is the most common genetic disorder of people with European ancestry. This disorder affects the exocrine system. A fibrous cyst is formed on the pancreas that blocks the pancreatic ducts. This causes sweat glands to release high levels of salt. A thick mucous is secreted from mucous glands that accumulates in the lungs. This accumulation of mucous causes bacterial infections and possibly death. Cystic fibrosis cannot be cured but can be treated for a short while. Most children with the disorder die before adulthood. Scientists identified a protein that transports chloride ions across cell membranes. Those with cystic fibrosis have a mutation in the gene coding for the protein. The majority of the mutant alleles have a deletion of the three nucleotides coding for phenylalanine at position 508. The other people with the disorder have mutant alleles caused by substitution, deletion, and frameshift mutations.

Skill 11.6   Identifying the role of nonnuclear inheritance (e.g., mitochondrial DNA) in phenotypic expression

Mitochondrial DNA is passed to the next generation by the mother. A genetic defect in the mother's mitochondrial DNA will pass to her offspring, regardless of the paternal DNA.

COMPETENCY 12.0 UNDERSTAND THE TECHNIQUES AND APPLICATIONS OF MODERN GENETICS.

Skill 12.1   Recognizing techniques used in the isolation, manipulation, and expression of genetic material (e.g., electrophoresis, DNA fingerprinting, recombinant DNA technology)

In its simplest form, genetic engineering requires enzymes to cut DNA, a vector, and a host organism for the recombinant DNA. A restriction enzyme is a bacterial enzyme that cuts foreign DNA in specific locations. The restriction fragment that results can be inserted into a bacterial plasmid (vector). Other vectors that may be used include viruses and bacteriophage. The splicing of restriction fragments into a plasmid results in a recombinant plasmid. This recombinant plasmid can now be placed in a host cell, usually a bacterial cell, and replicate.

The use of recombinant DNA provides a means to transplant genes among species. This opens the door for cloning specific genes of interest. Hybridization can be used to find a gene of interest. A probe is a molecule complementary in sequence to the gene of interest. The probe, once it has bonded to the gene, can be detected by labeling with a radioactive isotope or a fluorescent tag.

Gel electrophoresis is another method for analyzing DNA. Electrophoresis separates DNA or protein by size or electrical charge. The DNA runs towards the positive charge as it separates the DNA fragments by size. The gel is treated with a DNA-binding dye that fluoresces under ultraviolet light. A picture of the gel can be taken and used for analysis.

One of the most widely used genetic engineering techniques is polymerase chain reaction (PCR). PCR is a technique in which a piece of DNA can be amplified into billions of copies within a few hours. This process requires primer to specify the segment to be copied, and an enzyme (usually taq polymerase) to amplify the DNA. PCR has allowed scientists to perform several procedures on the smallest amount of DNA.

Deoxyribonucleic acid (DNA) is the genetic material found within the cell nucleus of all living organisms. DNA is made up of a double helix of two strands of nucleotide bases spiraled around each other. Each strand is composed of varying sequences of the four nucleotides adenine (A), guanine (G), cytosine (C) and thymine (T). Bonding at each nucleotide base pair connects the two strands of the double helix. Adenine bonds only to thymine and guanine bonds only to cytosine. With the exception of identical twins, no two people have the same sequence of base pairs. Every person can, therefore, be identified by the sequence of his or her base pairs. Genetic fingerprint or DNA fingerprint are terms for an individual's unique sequence of base pairs determined using molecular probes.

DNA fingerprinting is accomplished by first extracting a DNA sample from body tissue or fluid. DNA must be isolated from other cellular material in the nucleus through chemical precipitation reactions. DNA is then cut into several differently sized pieces using restriction enzymes, endonucleases that cleave double-stranded DNA only at particular nucleotide sequences. Cut DNA is sorted by fragment size using gel electrophoresis. In this process, DNA samples are placed in wells of agarose gel and exposed to electrical charge. The negative charge is applied closest to the wells containing the DNA, and the positive charge is applied farthest from the wells. Because DNA is negatively charged, DNA fragments migrate toward the positive charge. The smaller the DNA fragment, the faster its rate of migration. Thus, at the completion of gel electrophoresis, DNA fragments are sorted on the gel according to size.

Following electrophoresis, DNA undergoes a "Southern blot," a common method of analyzing genetic patterns that appear in an individual's DNA. In a Southern blot, double-stranded DNA contained in gel is denatured through heating or chemical treatment to produce single stranded DNA. Denatured DNA is then transferred from the gel to a nitrocellulose membrane using capillary action. The capillary apparatus is set up by placing the gel on top of a wick that lies over a buffer solution. The nitrocellulose membrane is placed on top of the gel, and then absorbent paper is placed on top of the membrane. The transfer process can be quickened using a vacuum blot apparatus. After capillary action has taken place, the gel and membrane are treated with UV light or baked to permanently attach DNA to the membrane through covalent boding.

The membrane and DNA are then incubated with a single-stranded DNA (ssDNA) probe that has been radioactively labeled. This probe preferentially binds to DNA according to base pair complementarity. After the radioactive probe has annealed to DNA on the membrane, an autoradiograph can be used to visualize results. Because each individual has unique base pair sequences, the radioactive probe binding pattern will be distinctive. X-ray films reveal only areas where the radioactive probe binds, portraying the occurrence and frequency of particular genetic pattern in person's DNA. This pattern can be used to definitively identify an individual.

Skill 12.2   Relating the applications of genetic engineering to medicine (e.g., gene therapy) and agriculture (e.g., transgenic crops)

Genetic engineering has made enormous contributions to medicine. Genetic engineering has opened the door to DNA technology. The use of DNA probes and polymerase chain reaction (PCR) has enabled scientists to identify and detect elusive pathogens. Diagnosis of genetic disease is now possible before the onset of symptoms.

Genetic engineering has allowed for the treatment of some genetic disorders. Gene therapy is the introduction of a normal allele to the somatic cells to replace the defective allele. The medical field has had success in treating patients with a single enzyme deficiency disease. Gene therapy has allowed doctors and scientists to introduce a normal allele that would provide the missing enzyme.

Insulin and mammalian growth hormones have been produced in bacteria by gene- splicing techniques. Insulin treatment helps control diabetes for millions of people who suffer from the disease. The insulin produced in genetically engineered bacteria is chemically identical to that made in the pancreas. Human grown hormone (HGH) has been genetically engineered for treatment of dwarfism caused by insufficient amounts of HGH. HGH is being further researched for treatment of broken bones and severe burns.

Biotechnology has advanced the techniques used to create vaccines. Genetic engineering allows for the modification of a pathogen in order to attenuate it for vaccine use. In fact, vaccines created by a pathogen attenuated by gene-splicing may be safer than using the traditional mutants.

Forensic scientists regularly use DNA technology to solve crimes. DNA testing can determine a person's guilt or innocence. A suspect's DNA fingerprint is compared to the DNA found at the crime scene. If the fingerprints match, guilt can then be established.

Many microorganisms are used to detoxify toxic chemicals and to recycle waste. Sewage treatment plants use microbes to degrade organic compounds. Some compounds, like chlorinated hydrocarbons, cannot be easily degraded. Scientists are working on genetically modifying microbes to be able to degrade the harmful compounds that the current microbes cannot.

Genetic engineering has benefited agriculture also. For example, many dairy cows are given bovine growth hormone to increase milk production. Commercially grown plants are often genetically modified for optimal growth.

Strains of wheat, cotton, and soybeans have been developed to resist herbicides used to control weeds. This allows for the successful growth of the plants while destroying the weeds. Crop plants are also being engineered to resist infections and pests. Scientists can genetically modify crops to contain a viral gene that does not affect the plant and will "vaccinate" the plant from a virus attack. Crop plants are now being modified to resist insect attacks. This allows for farmers to reduce the amount of pesticide used on plants.

COMPETENCY 13.0 UNDERSTAND CONCEPTS AND PRINCIPLES OF POPULATION GENETICS.

Skill 13.1 **Recognizing the concept of a gene pool, demonstrating knowledge of the concept of Hardy-Weinberg equilibrium and applying the Hardy-Weinberg equation to solve problems involving genotypic and phenotypic frequencies in populations**

The Hardy-Weinberg theory of gene equilibrium is a mathematical prediction to show shifting gene patterns. Let's use the letter "A" to represent the dominant condition of normal skin pigment. "a" would represent the recessive condition of albinism. In a population, there are three possible genotypes; AA, Aa and aa. AA and Aa would have normal skin pigment and only aa would be albinos. According to the Hardy-Weinberg law, there are five requirements to keep a gene frequency stable, leading to no evolution:

1. There is no mutation in the population.
2. There are no selection pressures; one gene is not more desirable in the environment.
3. There is no mating preference; mating is random.
4. The population is isolated; there is no immigration or emigration.
5. The population is large (mathematical probability is more correct with a large sample).

The above conditions are extremely difficult to meet. If these five conditions are not met, then gene frequency can shift, leading to evolution. Let's say in a population, 75% of the population has normal skin pigment (AA and Aa) and 25% are albino (aa). Using the following formula, we can determine the frequency of the A allele and the "a" allele in a population.

This can be used over generations to determine if evolution is occurring. The formula is: $1 = p^2 + 2pq + q^2$; where 1 is the total population. p^2 is the number of AA individuals, $2pq$ is the number of Aa individuals, and q^2 is the number of aa individuals.

Since you cannot tell by looking if an individual is AA or Aa, you must use the aa individuals to find that frequency first. As stated above aa was 25% of the population. Since $aa = q^2$, we can determine the value of q (or a) by finding the square root of 0.25, which is 0.5. Therefore, 0.5 of the population has the "a" gene. In order to find the value for p, use the following formula: $1 = p + q$. This would make the value of $p = 0.5$.

The gene pool is all the alleles at all gene loci in all individuals of a population. The Hardy-Weinberg theorem describes the gene pool in a non-evolving population. It states that the frequencies of alleles and genotypes in a population's gene pool are random unless acted on by something other than sexual recombination.

Now, to find the number of *AA*, plug it into the first formula;

$$AA = p^2 = 0.5 \times 0.5 = 0.25$$
$$Aa = 2pq = 2(0.5 \times 0.5) = 0.5$$
$$aa = q^2 = 0.5 \times 0.5 = 0.25$$

Any problem you may have with Hardy Weinberg will have an obvious squared number. The square of that number will be the frequency of the recessive gene, and you can figure anything else out knowing the formula and the frequency of *q*!

When frequencies vary from the Hardy Weinberg equilibrium, the population is said to be evolving. The change to the gene pool is on such a small scale that it is called microevolution.

Skill 13.2   Identifying factors that contribute to changing allele frequencies in a population

Certain factors increase the chances of variability in a population, thus leading to evolution. Items that increase variability include mutations, sexual reproduction, immigration, large population, and variation in geographic local. Changes that decrease variation would be natural selection, emigration, small population, and random mating.

Skill 13.3   Analyzing how new traits become established in populations

The environment can have an impact on phenotype. For example, a person living in a higher altitude will have a varying amount of red and white blood cells than those living at sea level.

In some cases, a particular trait is advantageous to the organism in a particular environment. Sickle-cell disease causes a low oxygen level in the blood which results in red blood cells having a sickle shape. About one in every ten African-Americans have the sickle-cell trait. These heterozygous carriers are usually healthy compared to homozygous individuals who can suffer severe detrimental effects. In the tropical Africa environment, a heterozygote is more resistant to malaria than those who do not carry any copies of the sickle-cell gene.

Skill 13.4   Recognizing populations as the units of evolution

Evolution currently is defined as a change in genotype over time. Gene frequencies shift and change from generation to generation. Populations evolve, not individuals.

COMPETENCY 14.0 UNDERSTAND PROCESSES OF EVOLUTIONARY CHANGE.

Skill 14.1   Recognizing the key points of Darwin's theory of evolution

There are two theories on the rate of evolution. Gradualism is the theory that minor evolutionary changes occur at a regular rate. Darwin's book, On the Origin of Species,, is based on this theory of gradualism. Charles Darwin was born in 1809 and spent 5 years in his twenties on a ship called the *Beagle*. Of all the locations the *Beagle* sailed to, it was the Galapagos Islands that infatuated Darwin. There he collected 13 species of finches that were quite similar. He could not accurately determine whether these finches were of the same species. He later learned these finches were in fact separate species. Darwin began to hypothesize that new species arose from its ancestors by the gradual collection of adaptations to a different environment. Darwin's most popular hypothesis is on the beak size of Galapagos finches. He theorized that the finches' beak sizes evolved to accommodate different food sources. Many people did not believe in Darwin's theories until recent field studies proved successful.

Although Darwin believed the origin of species was gradual, he was bewildered by the gaps in fossil records of living organisms. Punctuated equilibrium is the model of evolution that states that organismal form diverges and species form rapidly over relatively short periods of geological history, and then progress through long stages of stasis with little or no change. Punctuationalists use fossil records to support their claim. It is probable that both theories are correct, depending on the particular lineage studied.

Skill 14.2   Identifying sources of population variation on which natural selection can act (e.g., mutations, genetic drift)

Heritable variation is responsible for the individuality of organisms. An individual's phenotype is based on inherited genotype and the surrounding environment. For example, people can alter their phenotypes by lifting weight or diet and exercise.

Variation is generated by mutation and sexual recombination. Mutations may be errors in replication or a spontaneous rearrangement of one or more segments of DNA.

Mutations contribute a minimal amount of variation in a population. It is the unique recombination of existing alleles that causes the majority of genetic differences. Recombination is caused by the crossing over of the parents' genes during meiosis. This results in a unique offspring. With all the possible mating combinations in the world, it is obvious how sexual reproduction is the primary cause of genetic variation.

Genetic drift is another source of variation in a population. Genetic drift refers to the random inheritance of genes that are neither beneficial nor detrimental. Because the gene is neither a help nor a harm, it is not selected for or against in natural selection. As such, it continues to be passed down throughout generations. It is expected that over huge spans of time, a neutral gene would either be present in 100% or 0% of the population. This method of variation opposes natural selection. Genetic drift refers to the tendency of any allele to vary randomly in frequency over time due to statistical variation alone. Like selection, genetic drift acts on populations. Genetic drift is observed most strongly in small populations and results in changes that are not necessarily adaptations.

Skill 14.3   Analyzing the role of natural selection in leading to genotypic and phenotypic changes in a population over time

Natural selection is based on the survival of certain traits in a population through the course of time. The phrase "survival of the fittest," is often associated with natural selection. Fitness is the contribution an individual makes to the gene pool of the next generation.

Natural selection acts on phenotypes. An organism's phenotype is constantly exposed to its environment. Based on an organism's phenotype, selection indirectly adapts a population to its environment by maintaining favorable genotypes in the gene pool.

There are three modes of natural selection. Stabilizing selection favors the more common phenotypes, directional selection shifts the frequency of phenotypes in one direction, and diversifying selection occurs when individuals on both extremes of the phenotypic range are favored.

Sexual selection leads to the secondary sex characteristics between male and females. Animals that use mating behaviors may be successful or unsuccessful. An animal that lacks attractive plumage or has a weak mating call will not attract the female, thereby eventually limiting that gene in the gene pool. Mechanical isolation, where sex organs do not fit the female, has an obvious disadvantage.

Skill 14.4   Recognizing adaptations as products of selection of naturally occurring variations in populations

Variations occur naturally within a population. Some of these variations will aid an individual, others will harm, and still others will have no effect on one's survival. Those individuals with positive variations will best survive, and produce offspring that are more adapted to the environment. The colorations of plants and animals serve as camouflage or as warning in their environments. Cryptic coloration is that color or pattern that serves to conceal. For example, moths with light-colored wings are nearly invisible on birch trees (their chosen home), but are obvious to all birds, and therefore eaten, when they land on a dark tree trunk. In grasshoppers, only green ones are seen in areas where there is abundant lush grass but only tan and brown ones are seen in dry prairie areas. Those that do not match their environment do not survive to reproduce. Most animals (including many birds and insects) are darker on their backs than underneath. This tends to conceal them since most light comes from above and is absorbed by the darkness of their upper bodies.

According to the theory of cryptic coloration by natural selection animals have a hereditary variation in color and pattern. Some variations are more likely to deceive predators than others. Typically, predators will find and kill more of the less well-protected variants. This will leave a population in a given location that is better concealed and better protected.

On the other hand, many insects have unpleasant tastes, bristles, or stings that make them disagreeable as food. These do not help the insects if the predator does not know about them prior to killing and tasting that insect, so many also have colorations that serve to warn the predator.

Skill 14.5   Analyzing factors that contribute to speciation (e.g., geographic isolation, reproductive isolation)

The most commonly used species concept is the Biological Species Concept (BSC). This states that a species is a reproductive community of populations that occupy a specific niche in nature. It focuses on reproductive isolation of populations as the primary criterion for recognition of species status. The biological species concept does not apply to organisms that are completely asexual in their reproduction, fossil organisms, or distinctive populations that hybridize.

Reproductive isolation is caused by any factor that impedes two species from producing viable, fertile hybrids. Reproductive barriers can be categorized as prezygotic (premating) or postzygotic (postmating).

The prezygotic barriers are as follows:

1. Habitat isolation – species occupy different habitats in the same territory.
2. Temporal isolation – populations reaching sexual maturity/flowering at different times of the year.
3. Ethological isolation – behavioral differences that reduce or prevent interbreeding between individuals of different species (including pheromones and other attractants).
4. Mechanical isolation – structural differences that make gamete transfer difficult or impossible.
5. Gametic isolation – male and female gametes do not attract each other; no fertilization.

The postzygotic barriers are as follows:

Hybrid inviability – hybrids die before sexual maturity.
Hybrid sterility – disrupts gamete formation; no normal sex cells.
Hybrid breakdown – reduces viability or fertility in progeny of the F_2 backcross.

Geographical isolation can also lead to the origin of species. Allopatric speciation is speciation without geographic overlap. It is the accumulation of genetic differences through division of a species' range, either through a physical barrier separating the population or through expansion by dispersal such that gene flow is cut. In sympatric speciation, new species arise within the range of parent populations. Populations are sympatric if their geographical range overlaps. This usually involves the rapid accumulation of genetic differences (usually chromosomal rearrangements) that prevent interbreeding with adjacent populations.

Skill 14.6   Evaluating observations in various areas of biology in terms of evolutionary theory (e.g., embryology, biochemistry, molecular genetics)

1. Embryology:
Comparative embryology shows how embryos start off looking the same. As they develop, their similarities slowly decrease until they take the form of their particular class.

For example, adult vertebrates are diverse, yet their embryos are quite similar at very early stages. Fish like structures still form in early embryos of reptiles, birds, and mammals. In fish embryos, a two chambered heart, some veins, and parts of arteries develop and persist in adult fishes. The same structures form early in human embryos but do not persist as such in adults.

2. Biochemistry:

All known extant organisms make use of DNA and /or RNA. ATP is used as metabolic currency by all extant life. The genetic code is same for all organisms, meaning that a piece of RNA in a bacterium codes for the same protein as in a human cell.

A classic example of biochemical evidence for evolution is the variance of the protein Cytochrome c in living cells. The variance of Cytochrome c of different organisms is measured in the number of differing amino acids, each differing amino acid being a result of a base pair substitution, a mutation. If each differing amino acid is assumed to be the result of one base pair substitution, it can be calculated how long ago the two species diverged by multiplying the number of base pair substitutions by the estimated time it takes for a substituted base pair of the Cytochrome c gene to mutate in N thousand years, the number of amino acids making up the Cytochrome c protein in monkeys differ by one from that of humans, this leads us to believe that the two species diverged N million years ago.

3. Molecular genetics

Molecular genetics is the study of the structure and function of genes at the molecular level. The genetic structures and DNA sequences of an organism reveal the organism's evolutionary history. Scientists use tools of molecular genetics to study mutations in DNA that can lead to natural selection and evolution. The study of DNA using molecular genetic techniques provides us with statistics such as the 95% similarity between humans and chimpanzees.

There are many observations and examples in molecular genetics that show evolutionary relationships between organisms. For example, the amino acid sequence of Cytochrome c, a respiratory pigment found in eukaryotic cells, has changed slowly over time. Thus, when comparing two organisms, the amount of difference in the amino acid sequence of Cytochrome c estimates the degree of evolutionary relationship. The smaller the difference, the closer the relationship between the organisms. Humans and chimpanzees have identical Cytochrome c sequences, the difference between humans and rhesus monkeys is a single amino acid, the difference between humans and penguins is 11 amino acids, and the difference between humans and yeast is 38 amino acids. Such comparisons support the evolutionary theory that small changes in DNA sequence can lead to large diversions in lineages.

Another observation in molecular genetics related to evolutionary theory is the origin of mitochondria in eukaryotic cells. Studies and comparisons of mitochondrial DNA and bacterial DNA reveal a close relationship. From these observations, many scientists believe that mitochondria originated from free-living bacteria.

COMPETENCY 15.0 UNDERSTAND CHARACTERISTICS OF ANCIENT LIFE AND RELATED EVIDENCE.

Skill 15.1 Identifying theories regarding the origins and evolution of life

The hypothesis that life developed on Earth from nonliving materials is the most widely accepted theory on the origin of life. The transformation from nonliving materials to life had four stages. The first stage was the nonliving (abiotic) synthesis of small monomers such as amino acids and nucleotides. In the second stage, these monomers combine to form polymers, such as proteins and nucleic acids. The third stage is the accumulation of these polymers into droplets called protobionts. The last stage is the origin of heredity, with RNA as the first genetic material.

The first stage of this theory was hypothesized in the 1920s. A. I. Oparin and J. B. S. Haldane were the first to theorize that the primitive atmosphere was a reducing atmosphere with no oxygen present. The gases were rich in hydrogen, methane, water and ammonia.. In the 1950s, Stanley Miller proved Oparin's theory in the laboratory by combining the above gases. When given an electrical spark, he was able to synthesize simple amino acids. It is commonly accepted that amino acids appeared before DNA. Other laboratory experiments have supported the other stages in the origin of life theory could have happened.

Other scientists believe simpler hereditary systems originated before nucleic acids. In 1991, Julius Rebek was able to synthesize a simple organic molecule that replicates itself. According to his theory, this simple molecule may be the precursor of RNA.

Prokaryotes are the simplest life form. Their small genome size limits the number of genes that control metabolic activities. Over time, some prokaryotic groups became multicellular organisms for this reason. Prokaryotes then evolved to form complex bacterial communities where species benefit from one another.

The endosymbiotic theory of the origin of eukaryotes states that eukaryotes arose from symbiotic groups of prokaryotic cells. According to this theory, smaller prokaryotes lived within larger prokaryotic cells, eventually evolving into chloroplasts and mitochondria. Chloroplasts are the descendant of photosynthetic prokaryotes and mitochondria are likely to be the descendants of bacteria that were aerobic heterotrophs. Serial endosymbiosis is a sequence of endosymbiotic events. Serial endosymbiosis may also play a role in the progression of life forms to become eukaryotes.

Skill 15.2   Evaluating evidence from various areas of biology (e.g., paleontology, molecular genetics) regarding the origins of life and evolutionary relationships among major groups of organisms

Fossils are the key to understanding biological history. They are the preserved remnants left by an organism that lived in the past. Scientists have established the geological time scale to determine the age of a fossil. The geological time scale is broken down into four eras: the Precambrian, Paleozoic, Mesozoic, and Cenozoic. The eras are further broken down into periods that represent a distinct age in the history of Earth and its life. Scientists use rock layers called strata to date fossils. The older layers of rock are at the bottom. This allows scientists to correlate the rock layers with the era they date back to. Radiometric dating is a more precise method of dating fossils. Rocks and fossils contain isotopes of elements accumulated over time. The isotope's half-life is used to date older fossils by determining the amount of isotope remaining and comparing it to the half-life.

Dating fossils is helpful to construct and evolutionary tree. Scientists can arrange the succession of animals based on their fossil record. The fossils of an animal's ancestors can be dated and placed on its evolutionary tree. For example, the branched evolution of horses shows the progression of the modern horse's ancestors to be larger, to have a reduced number of toes, and have teeth modified for grazing.

The genetic code is a highly detailed historical record of the evolution of life forms. By studying molecular genetics, scientists can determine relationships between organisms. Organisms that share a large number of genetic sequences most likely have a common ancestor. Molecular studies have produced many interesting pieces of information about the evolutionary relationships between groups of organisms. For example, studies indicate that humans and mice share an ancestor that lived about 50 million years ago while humans and New World monkeys share an ancestor that lived 7 years ago. In addition, all humans share a common ancestor that lived 270,000 years ago. Similar studies exist that describe the evolutionary relationships among other groups of organisms. Finally, molecular genetics estimates that life originated on Earth about 3.5–3.8 billion years ago and all life descended from a primordial single-celled organism. Molecular genetics, however, cannot explain the origin of this original organism.

Skill 15.3   Evaluating the strengths and limitations of the fossil record

The fossil record is a rich source of evidence and information for the study of biological diversity, episodic speciation, and mass extinction.

Life on Earth is tremendously diverse and diversity continues to increase with time. Despite this colossal diversity, many seemingly unrelated species display a surprisingly large amount of structural similarity. For example, the skeletons of mice and humans are very similar. Such similarity between species indicates descent from a common ancestor, whose existence we can often confirm by studying the fossil record. In addition, evolutionary theory explains that biological diversity results from the adaptations of native or migrant predecessors to changing environments. Thus, the fossil record should provide evidence of common ancestors or proof of migration. And, in fact, studies of fossil layers indicate that the diversity and complexity of species has increased over time.

When studying the fossil record for evidence of evolution, biologists have noted that there are many gaps between species in suspected lineages. Biologists use the episodic nature of speciation to explain gaps in the fossil record. Gaps in the fossil record may indicate that evolution proceeds intermittently, not in a strictly gradual way. Small changes in a lineage that lead to eventual reproductive isolation and speciation may not show up in the fossil record. Thus, the changes of lineages seen in the fossil record are often the result of episodic speciation events.

Finally, scientists define a mass extinction event as a brief period where a large number of species become extinct. The fossil record indicates that there have been between five and fifteen mass extinction events in the Earth's history. Scientists look for the disappearance of multiple species from the fossil record during a single time period as evidence of a mass extinction event. This method of identification can be misleading, however, because other factors such as environmental changes can artificially erase species from the fossil record.

Skill 15.4 Recognizing characteristics of major extinction events in earth's history and evidence of their causes

Mass extinction events occur when the number of species sharply decreases in a relatively short period of time. Scientists recognize five key mass extinction events in the Earth's history.

- 440 million years ago (Ordovician period) – more than 100 families of organisms became extinct; many marine species became extinct due to glaciation and rising sea levels
- 360 million years ago (Devonian period) – a prolonged extinction event resulting in extinction of 70% of species
- 245 million years ago (Permian period) – resulted in extinction of 50% of all animal families, 95% of all marine species, and many tree species
- 208 million years ago (Triassic period) – resulted in extinction of 35% of all animal families including many of the early dinosaur families

- 65 million years ago (Cretaceous-Tertiary boundary) – about half of all life forms became extinct including the dinosaurs and many marine species

In addition to the "big five" mass extinction events, many scientists believe that the sixth major mass extinction event is currently underway.

Most scientists believe an impact event, a collision with a large asteroid or comet, caused the Cretaceous-Tertiary (C-T) mass extinction. Geochemical evidence supports this theory. Scientists have found evidence of an increase in elements found in extraterrestrial objects (e.g. iridium) in the Earth's surface dating to the time of the C-T extinction.

Geological studies also indicate that glaciation, climate change, anoxic events, and large volcanic eruptions caused the other mass extinction events. The geological record in temperate zones shows signs of cooling and glaciation around the times of the mass extinctions. Volcanic eruptions that caused climate change, warming of oceans, and a decrease in marine oxygen levels, likely played a role in many of the mass extinction events.

SUBAREA IV. **ORGANIZATION OF LIVING THINGS**

COMPETENCY 16.0 UNDERSTAND THE CHARACTERISTICS OF LIVING ORGANISMS AND HOW ORGANISMS ARE CLASSIFIED.

Skill 16.1   Identifying the characteristics of life and requirements needed to sustain life

Life has defining properties. Some of the more important processes and properties associated with life are as follows:

-Order – an organism's complex organization.
-Reproduction – life only comes from life (biogenesis).
-Energy utilization – organisms use and make energy to do many kinds of work.
-Growth and development – DNA directed growth and development.
-Adaptation to the environment – occurs by homeostasis (ability to maintain a certain status), response to stimuli, and evolution.

Life is highly organized. The organization of living systems builds on levels from small to increasingly more large and complex. All aspects, whether it is a cell or an ecosystem, have the same requirements to sustain life. Life is organized from simple to complex in the following way:

Atoms→molecules→organelles→cells→tissues→organs→organ systems→organism

Skill 16.2   Comparing living organisms and nonliving things

Living organisms exhibit the following things: order, reproduction, energy utilization, growth and development, and adaptation. Nonliving things do not have these properties. Let's look at how a human being is an example of a living being.

Humans are living organisms that display the basic properties of life. Humans share functional characteristics with all living organisms, from simple bacteria to complex mammals. The basic functions of living organisms include reproduction, growth and development, metabolism, and homeostasis/response to the environment.

Reproduction – All living organisms reproduce their own kind. Life arises only from other life. Humans reproduce through sexual reproduction, requiring the interaction of a male and a female. Human sexual reproduction is nearly identical to reproduction in other mammals. In addition, while simpler organisms have different methods of reproduction, they all reproduce. For example, the major mechanism of bacterial reproduction is asexual binary fission in which the cell divides in half, producing two identical cells.

Growth and Development – Growth and development, as directed by DNA, produces an organism characteristic of its species. In humans and other higher-level mammals, growth and development is a very complex process. In humans, growth and development requires differentiation of cells into many different types to form the various organs, structures, and functional elements. While differentiation is unique to higher level organisms, all living organisms grow. For example, the simplest bacterial cell grows in size until it divides into two organisms. Human body cells undergo a similar process, growing in size until division is necessary.

Metabolism – Metabolism is the sum of all chemical reactions that occur in a living organism. Catabolism is the breaking down of complex molecules to release energy. Anabolism is the utilization of the energy from catabolism to build complex molecules. Cellular respiration, the basic mechanism of catabolism in humans, is common to many living organisms of varying levels of complexity.

Homeostasis/Response to the Environment – All living organisms respond and adapt to their environments. Homeostasis is the result of regulatory mechanisms that help maintain an organism's internal environment within tolerable limits. For example, in humans and mammals, constriction and dilation of blood vessels near the skin help maintain body temperature.

Skill 16.3   Analyzing criteria used to classify organisms (e.g., morphology, genetic similarities, evolutionary relationships) and recognizing the hierarchical structure of the taxonomic system

It is believed that there are probably over ten million different species of living things. Of these, 1.5 million have been named and classified. Systems of classification show similarities and also assist scientists with a world wide system of organization.

Carolus Linnaeus is termed the father of taxonomy. Taxonomy is the science of classification. Linnaeus based his system on morphology (study of structure). Later on, evolutionary relationships (phylogeny) were also used to sort and group species. The modern classification system uses binomial nomenclature. This consists of a two word name for every species. The genus is the first part of the name and the species is the second part. Notice in the levels explained below that Homo sapiens is the scientific name for humans. Starting with the kingdom, the groups get smaller and more alike as one moves down the levels in the classification of humans:

Kingdom: Animalia, Phylum: Chordata, Subphylum: Vertebrata, Class: Mammalia, Order: Primate, Family: Hominidae, Genus: Homo, Species: sapiens

Species are defined by the ability to successfully reproduce with members of their own kind.

Several different morphological criteria are used to classify organisms:

1. Ancestral characters - characteristics that are unchanged after evolution (ie: 5 digits on the hand of an ape).

2. Derived characters - characteristics that have evolved more recently (ie: the absence of a tail on an ape).

3. Conservative characters - traits that change slowly.

4. Homologous characters - characteristics with the same genetic basis but used for a different function. (ie: wing of a bat, arm of a human. The bone structure is the same, but the limbs are used for different purposes).

5. Analogous characters – structures that differ, but used for similar purposes (ie- the wing of a bird and the wing of a butterfly).

6. Convergent evolution - development of similar adaptations by organisms that are unrelated.

Biological characteristics are also used to classify organisms. Protein comparison, DNA comparison, and analysis of fossilized DNA are powerful comparative methods used to measure evolutionary relationships between species. Taxonomists consider the organism's life history, biochemical (DNA) makeup, behavior, and how the organisms are distributed geographically. The fossil record is also used to show evolutionary relationships.

The current five kingdom system separates prokaryotes from eukaryotes. prokaryotes belong to the kingdom monera while the eukaryotes belong to either kingdom protista, plantae, fungi, or animalia. Recent comparisons of nucleic acids and proteins between different groups of organisms have led to problems concerning the five kingdom system. Based on these comparisons, alternative kingdom systems have emerged. Six and eight kingdoms as well as a three domain system have been proposed as a more accurate classification system. It is important to note that classification systems evolve as more information regarding characteristics and evolutionary histories of organisms arise.

Skill 16.4   Interpreting phylogenetic trees of related species

The typical graphic product of a classification is a phylogenetic tree, which represents a hypothesis of the relationships based on branching of lineages through time within a group. Every time you see a phylogenetic tree, you should be aware that it is making statements on the degree of similarity between organisms, or the particular pattern in which the various lineages diverged (phylogenetic history).

Cladistics is the study of phylogenetic relationships of organisms by analysis of shared, derived character states. Cladograms are constructed to show evolutionary pathways. Character states are polarized in cladistic analysis to be plesiomorphous (ancestral features), symplesiomorphous (shared ancestral features), apomorphous (derived characteristics), and synapomorphous (shared, derived features).

Skill 16.5   Classifying organisms based on given characteristics

Based upon characteristics of an organism, you should be able to at least define the large group to which it belongs. Here are some of the characteristics of the major kingdoms:

Kingdom Monera

Members of the Kingdom Monera are single-celled, prokaryotic organisms. Like all prokaryotes, Monerans lack nuclei and other membrane bound organelles, but do contain circular chromosomes and ribosomes. Most Monerans possess a cell wall made of peptidoglycan, a combination of sugars and proteins. Some Monerans also possess capsules and external motility devices (e.g. pili or flagella). The Kingdom Monera includes both eubacteria and archaebacteria. Though archaebacteria are structurally similar to eubacteria in many ways, there are key differences, like cell wall structure (archae lack peptidoglycan).

Kingdom Protista

Protists are eukaryotic, usually single-celled organisms (though some protists are multicellular). The Kingdom Protista is very diverse, containing members with characteristics of plants, animals, and fungi. All protists possess nuclei and some types of protists possess multiple nuclei. Most protists contain many mitochondria for energy production, and photosynthetic protists contain specialized structures called plastids where photosynthesis occurs. Motile protists possess external cilia or flagella. Finally, many protists have cell walls that do not contain cellulose.

Kingdom Fungi

Fungi are eukaryotic organisms that are mostly multicellular (single-celled yeast are the exception). Fungi possess cell walls composed of chitin. Fungal organelles are similar to animal organelles. Fungi are non-photosynthetic and possess neither chloroplasts nor plastids. Many fungal cells, like animal cells, possess centrioles. Fungi are also non-motile and release exoenzymes into the environment to dissolve food.

Kingdom Plantae

Plants are eukaryotic, multicellular, and have square-shaped cells. Plant cells possess rigid cell walls composed mostly of cellulose. Plant cells also contain chloroplasts and plastids for photosynthesis. Plant cells generally do not possess centrioles. Another distinguishing characteristic of plant cells is the presence of a large, central vacuole that occupies 50-90% of the cell interior. The vacuole stores acids, sugars, and wastes. Because of the presence of the vacuole, the cytoplasm is limited to a very small part of the cell.

Kingdom Animalia

Animals are eukaryotic, multicellular, and motile. Animal cells do not possess cell walls or plastids, but do possess a complex system of organelles. Most animal cells also possess centrioles, microtubule structures that play an important role in spindle formation during replication.

The three-domain system of classification, introduced by Carl Woese in 1990, emphasizes the separation of the two types of prokaryotes. The following is a comparison of the cellular characteristics of members of the three domains of living organisms: Eukarya, Bacteria, and Archaea.

Domain Eukarya

The Eukarya domain includes all members of the protist, fungi, plant, and animal kingdoms. Eukaryotic cells possess a membrane bound nucleus and other membranous organelles (e.g. mitochondria, Golgi, ribosomes). The chromosomes of Eukarya are linear and usually complexed with histones (protein spools). The cell membranes of eukaryotes consist of glycerol-ester lipids and sterols. The ribosomes of eukaryotes are 80 Svedburg (S) units in size. Finally, the cell walls of those eukaryotes that have them (i.e. plants, algae, fungi) are polysaccharide in nature.

Domain Bacteria

Prokaryotic members of the Kingdom Monera not classified as Archaea, are members of the Bacteria domain. Bacteria lack a defined nucleus and other membranous organelles. The ribosomes of bacteria measure 70 S units in size. The chromosome of Bacteria is usually a single, circular molecule that is not complexed with histones. The cell membranes of Bacteria lack sterols and consist of glycerol-ester lipids. Finally, most Bacteria possess a cell wall made of peptidoglycan.

Domain Archaea

Members of the Archaea domain are prokaryotic and similar to bacteria in most aspects of cell structure and metabolism. However, transcription and translation in Archaea are similar to the processes of eukaryotes, not bacteria. In addition, the cell membranes of Archaea consist of glycerol-ether lipids in contrast to the glycerol-ester lipids of eukaryotic and bacterial membranes. Finally, the cell walls of Archaea are not made of peptidoglycan, but consist of other polysaccharides, protein, and glycoprotein.

COMPETENCY 17.0 UNDERSTAND THE LIFE CYCLES OF ORGANISMS, INCLUDING REPRODUCTION, GROWTH, AND DEVELOPMENT.

Skill 17.1 Recognizing the characteristics of sexual and asexual reproduction

Sexual reproduction requires the genetic input from two different individuals. Asexual reproduction occurs within one individual who produces exact genetic copies of itself, usually through fission. The exception is that some bacteria can reproduce sexually through conjugation, where genetic material is exchanged. Sexual reproduction is a characteristic of higher level organisms. Animals reproduce sexually while bacteria reproduce asexually.

Skill 17.2 Comparing the relative advantages and disadvantages of sexual and asexual reproduction

The obvious advantage of asexual reproduction is that it does not require a partner. This is a huge advantage for organisms, such as the hydra, which do not move around. Not having to move around to reproduce also allows organisms to conserve energy. Asexual reproduction also tends to be faster. There are disadvantages, as in the case of regeneration, in plants if the plant is not in good condition or in the case of spore-producing plants, if the surrounding conditions are not suitable for the spores to grow. Asexual reproduction does not allow for genetic variation, which means that mutations, or weaker qualities, will be passed on. This can also be detrimental to a species well-adapted to a particular environment when the conditions of that environment change suddenly. On the whole, asexual reproduction is more reliable because it requires fewer steps and less can go wrong.

Sexual reproduction shares genetic information between gametes, thereby producing variety in the species. This can result in a better species with an improved chance of survival. There is the disadvantage that sexual reproduction requires a partner, which in turn with many organisms requires courtship, finding a mate, and mating. Another disadvantage is that sexually reproductive organisms require special mechanisms.

Skill 17.3   Analyzing the reproductive strategies of various organisms

Bacteria reproduce by binary fission. This asexual process is simply dividing the bacterium in half. All new organisms are exact clones of the parent.

Porifera - the sponges. They may reproduce sexually (either by cross or self fertilization) or asexually (by budding).

Cnidaria (Coelenterata) - the jellyfish. They may reproduce asexually (by budding) or sexually.

Platyhelminthes - the flatworms. They can reproduce asexually (by regeneration) or sexually. They may be hermaphroditic and possess both sex organs but cannot fertilize themselves.

Nematoda - the roundworms. They reproduce sexually with male and female worms.

Annelida - the segmented worms. They are hermaphroditic and each worm fertilizes the other upon mating.

Reproduction by plants is accomplished through alternation of generations. Simply stated, a haploid stage in the plants life history alternates with a diploid stage. The diploid sporophyte divides by meiosis to reduce the chromosome number to the haploid gametophyte generation. The haploid gametophytes undergo mitosis to produce gametes (sperm and eggs). Then, the haploid gametes fertilize to return to the diploid sporophyte stage.

The non-vascular plants need water to reproduce. The vascular non-seeded plants reproduce with spores and also need water to reproduce. Gymnosperms use seeds for reproduction and do not require water.

Angiosperms are the most numerous and are therefore the main focus of reproduction in this section. The sporophyte is the dominant phase in reproduction. Angiosperm reproductive structures are the flowers.

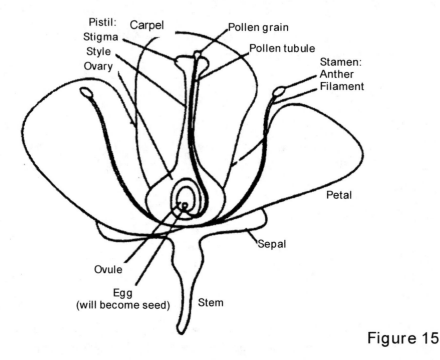

Figure 15

The male gametophytes are pollen grains and the female gametophytes are embryo sacs that are inside of the ovules. The male pollen grains are formed in the anthers at the tips of the stamens. The female ovules are enclosed by the ovaries. Therefore, the stamen is the reproductive organ of the male and the carpel is the reproductive organ of the female.

In a process called pollination, the pollen grains are released from the anthers and carried by animals and the wind and land on the carpels. The sperm is released to fertilize the eggs. Angiosperms reproduce through a method of double fertilization. An ovum is fertilized by two sperm. One sperm produces the new plant and the other forms the food supply for the developing plant (endosperm). The ovule develops into a seed and the ovary develops into a fruit. The fruit is then carried by wind or animals and the seeds are dispersed to form new plants.

Skill 17.4   Recognizing characteristics of developing embryos of plants and animals and the processes related to development (e.g., cleavage, gastrulation)

Animals

Animal tissue becomes specialized during development. The ectoderm (outer layer) becomes the epidermis or skin. The mesoderm (middle layer) becomes muscles and other organs beside the gut. The endoderm (inner layer) becomes the gut, also called the archenteron.

Sponges are the simplest animals and lack true tissue. They exhibit no symmetry.

Diploblastic animals have only two germ layers: the ectoderm and endoderm. They have no true digestive system. Diploblastic animals include the Cnideria (jellyfish).   They exhibit radial symmetry.

Triploblastic animals have all three germ layers. Triploblastic animals can be further divided into:

Acoelomates - have no defined body cavity. An example is the flatworm (Platyhelminthe), which must absorb food from a host's digestive system.

Pseudocoelomates - have a body cavity but it is not lined by tissue from the mesoderm. An example is the roundworm (Nematoda).

Coelomates - have a true fluid filled body cavity called a coelom derived from the mesoderm. Coelomates can further be divided into protostomes and deuterostomes. In the development of protostomes, the first opening becomes the mouth and the second opening becomes the anus. The mesoderm splits to form the coelom. In the development of deuterostomes, the mouth develops from the second opening and the anus from the first opening. The mesoderm hollows out to become the coelom. Protostomes include animals in phylums Mollusca, Annelida and Arthropoda. Deuterostomes include animals in phylums Ehinodermata and Vertebrata.

Development is defined as a change in form. Animals go through several stages of development after fertilization of the egg cell:

Cleavage - the first divisions of the fertilized egg. Cleavage continues until the egg becomes a blastula.

Blastula - the blastula is a hollow ball of undifferentiated cells.

Gastrulation - this is the time of tissue differentiation into the separate germ layers, the endoderm, mesoderm and ectoderm.

Neurulation - development of the nervous system.

Organogenesis - the development of the various organs of the body.

Plants

The development of the egg to form a plant occurs in three stages: growth; morphogenesis, the development of form, and cellular differentiation, the acquisition of a cell's specific structure and function.

Skill 17.5   **Demonstrating knowledge of the life cycles of familiar organisms (e.g., bacteria, flowering plants, amphibians, insects)**

Typical fungus: fruiting body -> spores formed by fertilization inside fruiting body -> spores released -> hypha -> fruiting body

Typical plant without flowers: sporophyte -> spores -> gametophyte -> sperm cell, egg cell -> fertilization -> zygote beneath gametophyte -> sporophyte

Typical conifer: adult tree -> ovule, pollen -> fertilization -> cone with seed inside -> adult tree

Typical flowering plant: adult plant -> ovule, pollen -> fertilization -> seed -> adult plant

Typical cnidarian: polyp -> medusa -> egg cell, sperm cell -> fertilization outside body -> larva -> polyp

Typical annelid worm: adult -> egg cell, sperm cell -> fertilization outside body -> eggs -> larva -> adult

Typical crustacean: adult -> egg cell, sperm cell -> fertilization outside body -> eggs -> larva -> adult

Typical insect: adult -> egg cell, sperm cell -> fertilization inside body -> eggs -> larva -> pupa -> adult

Typical bony fish: adult -> egg cell, sperm cell -> fertilization outside body -> eggs -> adult

Typical amphibian: adult -> egg cell, sperm cell -> fertilization outside body -> eggs (spawn) -> tadpole larva -> adult

Typical reptile: adult -> egg cell, sperm cell -> fertilization inside the body -> shelled egg -> adult

Typical bird: adult -> egg cell, sperm cell -> fertilization inside body -> shelled egg -> adult

Typical mammal: adult -> egg cell, sperm cell -> fertilization inside body -> fertilized egg develops inside body -> adult

COMPETENCY 18.0 UNDERSTAND THE STRUCTURES, ORGANIZATION, AND FUNCTIONS OF SYSTEMS IN ORGANISMS.

Skill 18.1 Recognizing levels of organization in multicellular organisms and the relationships among the levels (i.e., cells, tissues, organs, systems)

The levels of organization are as follows:
Atoms→molecules→organelles→cells→tissues→organs→organ systems→organism.

Each level of organization depends upon the previous level. Organization increases in both complexity and size as one moves up through the levels. This high degree of complexity explains why advanced animals have been able to grow so large and be successful.

Groups of related organs are organ systems. Organ systems consist of organs working together to perform a common function. The commonly recognized organ systems of animals include the reproductive system, nervous system, circulatory system, respiratory system, lymphatic system (immune system), endocrine system, urinary system, muscular system, digestive system, integumentary system, and skeletal system. In addition, organ systems are interconnected and a single system rarely works alone to complete a task.

One obvious example of the interconnectedness of organ systems is the relationship between the circulatory and respiratory systems. As blood circulates through the organs of the circulatory systems, it is re-oxygenated in the lungs of the respiratory system. Another example is the influence of the endocrine system on other organ systems. Hormones released by the endocrine system greatly influence processes of many organ systems including the nervous and reproductive systems.

In addition, bodily response to infection is a coordinated effort of the lymphatic (immune system) and circulatory systems. The lymphatic system produces specialized immune cells, filters out disease-causing organisms, and removes fluid waste from in and around tissue. The lymphatic system utilizes capillary structures of the circulatory system and interacts with blood cells in a coordinated response to infection.

Finally, the muscular and skeletal systems are closely related. Skeletal muscles attach to the bones of the skeleton and drive movement of the body.

Skill 18.2   Comparing the organization and structures of diverse life forms, from single celled to complex multicellular organisms

Single celled

Protists are the earliest eukaryotic descendants of prokaryotes. Protists are found almost anywhere there is water. Protists can be broadly defined as the eukaryotic microorganisms and include the macroscopic algae with only a single tissue type. They are defined by exclusion of characteristics common of the other kingdoms. They are not prokaryotes because they have (usually) a true nucleus and membrane bound organelles. They are not fungi because fungi lack undulopidia and develop from spores. They are not plants because plants develop from embryos, and they are not animals because animals develop from a blastula.

Most protists have a true (membrane-bound) nucleus, complex organelles (mitochondria, chloroplasts, etc.), aerobic respiration in mitochondria, and undulipodium (cilia) in some life stage.

The chaotic status of names and concepts of the higher classification of the protists reflects their great diversity of form, function, and life cycles. The protists are often grouped as algae (plant-like), protozoa (animal-like), or fungus-like, based on the similarity of their lifestyle and characteristics to these more derived groups. Two distinctive groups of protists are considered for separation as their own kingdoms. The Archaezoa lack mitochondria, the Golgi apparatus, and have multiple nuclei. The Chromista, including diatoms, brown algae and "golden" algae with chlorophyll *c*, have a very different photosynthetic plastid from those found in the green algae and plants.

Multi cellular

Animals constantly require oxygen for cellular respiration and need to remove carbon dioxide from their bodies. The respiratory surface must be large and moist. Different animal groups have different types of respiratory organs to perform gas exchange. Some animals use their entire outer skin for respiration (as in the case of worms). Fishes and other aquatic animals have gills for gas exchange. Ventilation increases the flow of water over the gills. This process brings oxygen and removes carbon dioxide through the gills. Fish use a large amount of energy to ventilate its gills. This is because the oxygen available in water is less than that available in the air. The arthropoda (insects) have tracheal tubes that send air to all parts of their bodies. Gas exchange for smaller insects is provided by diffusion. Larger insects ventilate their bodies by a series of body movements that compress and expand the tracheal tubes. Vertebrates have lungs as their primary respiratory organ. The gas exchange system in all vertebrates is similar to that in humans discussed in a later section.

Osmoregulation and excretion in many invertebrates involves tubular systems. The tubules branch throughout the body. Interstitial fluid enters these tubes and is collected into excretory ducts that empty into the external environment by openings in the body wall. Insects have excretory organs called Malpighian tubes. These organs pump water, salts, and nitrogenous waste into the tubules. These fluids then pass through the hindgut and out the rectum. Vertebrates have kidneys as the primary excretion organ.

Skill 18.3   Analyzing anatomical structures and physiological processes of body systems in various organisms (e.g., plants, invertebrates, vertebrates)

Animals constantly require oxygen for cellular respiration and need to remove carbon dioxide from their bodies. The respiratory surface must be large and moist. Different animal groups have different types of respiratory organs to perform gas exchange. Some animals use their entire outer skin for respiration (as in the case of worms).

Fishes and other aquatic animals have gills for gas exchange. Ventilation increases the flow of water over the gills. This process brings oxygen and removes carbon dioxide through the gills. Fish use a large amount of energy to ventilate its gills. This is because the oxygen available in water is less than that available in the air. The arthropoda (insects) have tracheal tubes that send air to all parts of their bodies.

Gas exchange for smaller insects is provided by diffusion. Larger insects ventilate their bodies by a series of body movements that compress and expand the tracheal tubes.

Vertebrates have lungs as their primary respiratory organ. The gas exchange system in all vertebrates is similar to that in humans discussed in a later section.

Osmoregulation and excretion in many invertebrates involves tubular systems. The tubules branch throughout the body. Interstitial fluid enters these tubes and is collected into excretory ducts that empty into the external environment by openings in the body wall. Insects have excretory organs called Malpighian tubes. These organs pump water, salts, and nitrogenous waste into the tubules. These fluids then pass through the hindgut and out the rectum. Vertebrates have kidneys as the primary excretion organ. This system is described in a later section.

Most of the large, complex plants are termed vascular plants because they possess specialized tissues to transport water. Vascular plants include ferns, clubmosses, horsetails, all flowering plants, conifers and gymnosperms. Remember that plants synthesize glucose through photosynthesis in their leaves and obtain water and certain nutrients (nitrogen, phosphorus) through their roots. Thus, the vascular system in plants consists of xylem and phloem. The xylem carries water and inorganic solutes up from the roots, while the phloem carries the organic solutes (mostly sugars) from the leaves to the rest of the plant. Note that there are certain simple plants, such as mosses, liverworts, and hornworts that are nonvascular. These plants must rely on diffusion alone to distribute water and nutrients. Therefore, the size that these plants may grow to is limited.

Skill 18.4   Relating the function of a body part or system to its structure or organization

Structure correlates with function in living organisms: structure follows function. By analyzing a biological structure you can postulate its function. For example, the bones in a bird's wings have a strong, light honeycomb structure. One can theorize that this structure contributes to the flight of the bird. Another example is the incisors of meat eating animals. These sharp teeth allow for ease in tearing off flesh from their prey. An example at the subcellular level is the extensive folding of the inner membrane of the mitochondria allows for a greater amount of this membrane to fit into the very small organelle.

Skill 18.5   Evaluating the adaptive significance of given structures or physiological processes

Plants require adaptations that allow them to absorb light for photosynthesis. Since they are unable to move about, they must evolve methods to allow them to successfully reproduce. As time passed, the plants moved from a water environment to the land. Advantages of life on land included more available light and a higher concentration of carbon dioxide. Originally, there were no predators and less competition for space on land. Plants had to evolve methods of support, reproduction, respiration, and conservation of water once they moved to land. Reproduction by plants is accomplished through alternation of generations. Simply stated, a haploid stage in the plants life history alternates with a diploid stage. A division of labor among plant tissues evolved in order to get water and minerals from the earth as described in the previous section. A wax cuticle is produced to prevent the loss of water. Leaves enabled plants to capture light and carbon dioxide for photosynthesis. Stomata provide openings on the underside of leaves for oxygen to move in or out of the plant and for carbon dioxide to move in. A method of anchorage (roots) evolved. The polymer lignin evolved to give tremendous strength to plants.

COMPETENCY 19.0   ANALYZE PROCESSES USED BY ORGANISMS TO OBTAIN, STORE, AND USE MATTER AND ENERGY AND TO MAINTAIN HOMEOSTASIS.

Skill 19.1   Understanding the need for organisms to obtain energy and cycle matter and comparing the processes by which different organisms do so

All organisms can be classed by the manner in which they obtain energy: chemoautotrophs, photoautotrophs, and heterotrophs.

Chemoautotrophs- These organisms are able to obtain energy via the oxidation of inorganic molecules (i.e., hydrogen gas and hydrogen sulfide) or methane. This process is known as chemosynthesis. Most chemoautotrophs are bacteria or archaea that thrive in oxygen-poor environments, such as deep sea vents.

Photoautotrophs- Instead of obtaining energy from simple inorganic compounds like the chemoautotrophs, organisms of this type receive energy from sunlight. They employ the process of photosynthesis to create sugar from light, carbon dioxide and water. Most higher plants and algae as well as some bacteria and protists are photoautotrophs.

Heterotrophs- Any organism that requires organic molecules as its source of energy is a heterotroph. These organisms are consumers in the food chain and must obtain nutrition from autotrophs or other heterotrophs. All animals are heterotrophs, as are some fungi and bacteria.

Skill 19.2   Identifying structures and processes used by organisms to store food and energy

Vacuoles are one of the most common storage compartments used by simple organisms and plants. Though we commonly think of vacuoles as simply the organelle employed by plant cells to maintain turgor pressure, they actually have a variety of functions. For example, in budding yeast cells, vacuoles are used as storage compartments for amino acids. When the yeast cells are deprived of food, proteins are consumed within the vacuoles. This process is known as autophagy. Additionally, protists and macrophages use vacuoles to hold food when they engage in phagocytosis (the cellular intake of large molecules or other cells).

Plants have evolved various methods to store excess food. While some store extra glucose, many plants store starch in their roots and stems. Seeds are often "packaged" with additional stored food in the form of both sugar and starch. Many common examples of such plant "storage devices" are exploited as food by humans. For instance, carrots are large roots packed with the plant's extra food. Most fruits, nuts, and edible seeds also contain many calories intended to nurture the next generation of plants.

In many animals, adipose (fat) tissue is used to store extra metabolic energy for long periods. Excess calories are metabolized by the liver into fat. This, along with dietary fat, is stored by adipocytes. When this energy is needed by the body, the stored fat can supply be broken down to supply fatty acids and glycerol. Glycerol can be converted to glucose and used as a source of energy for many cells in the body, while fatty acids are especially needed by the heart and skeletal muscle. The storage and use of this fat is under the control of several hormones including insulin, glucagons, and epinephrine.

Skill 19.3   Analyzing systems and processes involved in the distribution of nutrients to all parts of an organism

Complex, multi-cellular organisms must have systems to distribute nutrients to all their various tissues. The following describes these systems in plants and animals.

Plants

Roots absorb water and minerals and exchange gases in the soil. The xylem transports water and minerals, called xylem sap, upwards. This is pulled upwards in a process called transpiration. Transpiration is the evaporation of water from leaves. Gases are exchanged through the leaves and photosynthesis occurs. The sugar produced by photosynthesis goes down the phloem in the phloem sap. This sap is transported to the roots and other non-photosynthetic parts of the plant.

Note that there are certain simple plants, such as mosses, liverworts, and hornworts that are nonvascular. These plants must rely on diffusion alone to distribute water and nutrients. Therefore, the size that these plants may grow to is limited.

Animals

The equivalent of plants' xylem/phloem system in animals is the circulatory system. As in plants, the very simplest animals are nonvascular. Flatworms, for instance, lack circulatory systems. Their mouths lead directly to highly branched digestive systems. Nutrients, water, and gas simply diffuse from the digestive system into all the cells in the flatworm. Relying on diffusion alone to transport nutrients, of course, limits the size and complexity of organisms.
The circulatory system in any animal serves to deliver gases (oxygen) as well as nutrients from the digestive system to all the tissues of the body.
Certain animals, including mollusks and arthropods, possess open circulatory systems. The circulatory fluid, called hemolymph, in these animals is rather like a combination of the blood and interstitial fluid present in higher species.

The heart pumps the hemolymph into a fairly large, open cavity called the hemocoel. In the hemocoel, the hemolymph directly bathes all the animal's tissues and delivers nutrients. The hemolymph is composed of water, electrolytes, and organic compounds (carbohydrates, proteins, etc).

Higher species have closed circulatory systems, in which blood is always contained within arteries, capillaries, and veins. In these systems, the blood passes through tiny capillaries in the lungs and small intestines and absorbs oxygen and nutrients, respectively. The blood is pumped to all the tissues of the body, where the oxygen and nutrients diffuse out through more tiny capillaries. In general, arteries take oxygen and nutrients to the tissues, while veins return the blood to the heart. The various species have developed closed circulatory systems of varying complexity. Fish, for example have only a two chambered heart, while amphibians have three chambered hearts. Birds and mammals, however, have 4 chambered hearts, allowing complete separation between blood being pumped to and from the body and blood pumped to and from the lungs.

Skill 19.4 Recognizing the sources of energy used by various organisms (e.g., archaebacteria, plants, animals)

Autotrophs obtain the bulk of their food via either photosynthesis or chemosynthesis, which are anabolic processes. The organisms may also absorb some additional simple nutrients from the environment, such as the water and nitrogen plants take up through their roots. Heterotrophs, on the other hand, typically obtain complex organic nutrients by consuming autotrophs or other heterotrophs.

Skill 19.5 Analyzing anatomical structures, physiological responses, and behaviors that are involved in maintaining homeostasis

The molecular composition of the immediate environment outside of the organism is not the same as it is inside and the temperature outside may not be optimal for metabolic activity within the organism. Homeostasis is the control of these differences between internal and external environments. There are three homeostatic systems to regulate these differences.

Osmoregulation deals with maintenance of the appropriate level of water and salts in body fluids for optimum cellular functions. Excretion is the elimination of metabolic waste products from the body including excess water. Thermoregulation maintains the internal, or core, body temperature of the organism within a tolerable range for metabolic and cellular processes.

COMPETENCY 20.0 UNDERSTAND HUMAN ANATOMY AND PHYSIOLOGY.

Skill 20.1   Identifying structures and functions of the various body systems

Muscular system

The muscular system's function is for movement. There are three types of muscle tissue. Skeletal muscle is voluntary. These muscles are attached to bones and are responsible for their movement. Skeletal muscle consists of long fibers and is striated due to the repeating patterns of the myofilaments (made of the proteins actin and myosin) that make up the fibers.

Cardiac muscle is found in the heart. Cardiac muscle is striated like skeletal muscle, but differs in that plasma membrane of the cardiac muscle causes the muscle to beat even when away from the heart. The action potentials of cardiac and skeletal muscles also differ.

Smooth muscle is involuntary. It is found in organs and enable functions such as digestion and respiration. Unlike skeletal and cardiac muscle, smooth muscle is not striated. Smooth muscle has less myosin and does not generate as much tension as the striated muscles.

The axial skeleton consists of the bones of the skull and vertebrae. The appendicular skeleton consists of the bones of the legs, arms and tail, and shoulder girdle. Bone is a connective tissue. Parts of the bone include compact bone which gives strength, spongy bone which contains red marrow to make blood cells, yellow marrow in the center of long bones to store fat cells, and the periosteum which is the protective covering on the outside of the bone.

A joint is defined as a place where two bones meet. Joints enable movement. Ligaments attach bone to bone. Tendons attach bone to muscle. Joints allow great flexibility in movement. There are three types of joints:

1. Ball and socket – allows for rotation movement. An example is the joint between the shoulder and the humerus. This joint allows humans to move their arms and legs in many different ways.
2. Hinge – movement is restricted to a single plane. An example is the joint between the humerus and the ulna.
3. Pivot – allows for the rotation of the forearm at the elbow and the hands at the wrist.

A nerve impulse strikes a muscle fiber. This causes calcium ions to flood the sarcomere. Calcium ions allow ATP to expend energy. The myosin fibers creep along the actin, causing the muscle to contract. Once the nerve impulse has passed, calcium is pumped out and the contraction ends.

Skin

The skin consists of two distinct layers. The epidermis is the thinner outer layer and the dermis is the thicker inner layer. Layers of tightly packed epithelial cells make up the epidermis. The tight packaging of the epithelial cells supports the skin's function as a protective barrier against infection.

The top layer of the epidermis consists of dead skin cells and is filled with keratin, a waterproofing protein. The dermis layer consists of connective tissue. It contains blood vessels, hair follicles, sweat glands, and sebaceous glands. An oily secretion called sebum, produced by the sebaceous gland, is released to the outer epidermis through the hair follicles. Sebum maintains the pH of the skin between 3 and 5, which inhibits most microorganism growth.

The skin also plays a role in thermoregulation. Increased body temperature causes skin blood vessels to dilate, resulting in heat radiating from the skin's surface. The sweat glands are also activated, increasing evaporative cooling. Decreased body temperature causes skin blood vessels to constrict. This results in blood from the skin diverting to deeper tissues and reduces heat loss from the surface of the skin.

Respiratory system

The lungs are the respiratory surface of the human respiratory system. A dense net of capillaries contained just beneath the epithelium form the respiratory surface. The surface area of the epithelium is about $100m^2$ in humans. Based on the surface area, the volume of air inhaled and exhaled is the tidal volume. This is normally about 500mL in adults. Vital capacity is the maximum volume the lungs can inhale and exhale. This is usually around 3400mL.

Excretory system

The kidneys are the primary organ in the excretory system. The pair of kidneys in humans are about 10cm long each. They receive about 20% of the blood pumped with each heartbeat despite their small size. The function of the excretory system is to rid the body of nitrogenous wastes in the form of urea.

Circulatory system

The function of the closed circulatory system (cardiovascular system) is to carry oxygenated blood and nutrients to all cells of the body and return carbon dioxide waste to be expelled from the lungs. The heart, blood vessels, and blood make up the cardiovascular system. The structure of the heart is shown below:

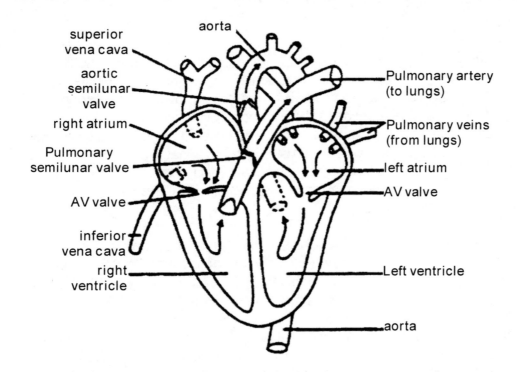

The atria are the chambers that receive blood returning to the heart and the ventricles are the chambers that pump blood out of the heart. There are four valves, two atrioventricular (AV) valves and two semilunar valves. The AV valves are located between each atrium and ventricle. The contraction of the ventricles closes the AV valve to keep blood from flowing back into the atria. The semilunar valves are located where the aorta leaves the left ventricle and the pulmonary artery leaves the right ventricle. The semilunar valves are opened by ventricular contraction to allow blood to be pumped out into the arteries and closed by the relaxation of the ventricles.

The cardiac output is the volume of blood per minute that the left ventricle pumps. This output depends on the heart rate and stroke volume. The heart rate is the number of times the heart beats per minute and the stroke volume is the amount of blood pumped by the left ventricle each time it contracts. Humans have an average cardiac output of about 5.25 L/min. Heavy exercise can increase cardiac output up to five times. Epinephrine and increased body temperature also increase heart rate and thus the cardiac output.

Cardiac muscle can contract without any signal from the nervous system. It is the sinoatrial node that is the pacemaker of the heart. It is located on the wall of the right atrium and generates electrical impulses that make the cardiac muscle cells contract in unison. The atrioventricular node shortly delays the electrical impulse to ensure the atria empty before the ventricles contract.

Nervous system

The central nervous system (CNS) consists of the brain and spinal cord. The CNS is responsible for the body's response to environmental stimulation. The spinal cord is located inside the spine. It sends out motor commands for movement in response to stimuli. The brain is where responses to more complex stimuli occurs. The meninges are the connective tissues that protect the CNS. The CNS contains fluid filled spaces called ventricles. These ventricles are filled when cerebrospinal fluid which is formed in the brain. This fluid cushions the brain and circulates nutrients, white blood cells, and hormones. The CNS's response to stimuli is a reflex. The reflex is an unconscious, automatic response.

The peripheral nervous system (PNS) consists of the nerves that connect the CNS to the rest of the body. The sensory division brings information to the CNS from sensory receptors and the motor division sends signals from the CNS to effector cells. The motor division consists of somatic nervous system and the autonomic nervous system. The somatic nervous system is controlled consciously in response to external stimuli. The autonomic nervous system is unconsciously controlled by the hypothalamus of the brain to regulate the internal environment. This system is responsible for the movement of smooth and cardiac muscles as well as the muscles for other organ systems.

The neuron is the basic unit of the nervous system. It consists of an axon, which carries impulses away from the cell body to the tip of the neuron; the dendrite, which carries impulses toward the cell body; and the cell body, which contains the nucleus. Synapses are spaces between neurons. Chemicals called neurotransmitters are found close to the synapse. The myelin sheath, composed of Schwann cells cover the neurons and provide insulation.

Nerve action depends on depolarization and an imbalance of electrical charges across the neuron. A polarized nerve has a positive charge outside the neuron. A depolarized nerve has a negative charge outside the neuron. Neurotransmitters turn off the sodium pump which results in depolarization of the membrane. This wave of depolarization (as it moves from neuron to neuron) carries an electrical impulse. This is actually a wave of opening and closing gates that allows for the flow of ions across the synapse. Nerves have an action potential. There is a threshold of the level of chemicals that must be met or exceeded in order for muscles to respond. This is called the "all or none" response.

Endocrine system

The function of the endocrine system is to manufacture proteins called hormones. Hormones are released into the bloodstream and are carried to a target tissue where they stimulate an action. There are two classes of hormones. Steroid hormones come from cholesterol and include the sex hormones. Peptide hormones are derived from amino acids. Hormones are specific and fit receptors on the target tissue cell surface. The receptor activates an enzyme that converts ATP to cyclic AMP. Cyclic AMP (cAMP) is a second messenger from the cell membrane to the nucleus. The genes found in the nucleus turn on or off to cause a specific response.

Hormones are secreted by endocrine cells which make up endocrine glands. The major endocrine glands and their hormones are as follows:

> Hypothalamus – located in the lower brain; signals the pituitary gland.
> Pituitary gland – located at the base of the hypothalamus; releases growth hormones and antidiuretic hormone (retention of water in kidneys).
> Thyroid gland – located on the trachea; lowers blood calcium levels (calcitonin) and maintains metabolic processes (thyroxine).
> Gonads – located in the testes of the male and the ovaries of the female; testes release androgens to support sperm formation and ovaries release estrogens to stimulate uterine lining growth and progesterone to promote uterine lining growth.
> Pancreas – secretes insulin to lower blood glucose levels and glucagon to raise blood glucose levels.

Skill 20.2   Recognizing the interrelationships of the different systems

Groups of related organs are organ systems. Organ systems consist of organs working together to perform a common function. The commonly recognized organ systems of animals include the reproductive system, nervous system, circulatory system, respiratory system, lymphatic system (immune system), endocrine system, urinary system, muscular system, digestive system, integumentary system, and skeletal system. In addition, organ systems are interconnected and a single system rarely works alone to complete a task.

One obvious example of the interconnectedness of organ systems is the relationship between the circulatory and respiratory systems. As blood circulates through the organs of the circulatory systems, it is re-oxygenated in the lungs of the respiratory system. Another example is the influence of the endocrine system on other organ systems. Hormones released by the endocrine system greatly influence processes of many organ systems including the nervous and reproductive systems.

In addition, bodily response to infection is a coordinated effort of the lymphatic (immune system) and circulatory systems. The lymphatic system produces specialized immune cells, filters out disease-causing organisms, and removes fluid waste from in and around tissue. The lymphatic system utilizes capillary structures of the circulatory system and interacts with blood cells in a coordinated response to infection.

The thyroid gland produces hormones that help maintain heart rate, blood pressure, muscle tone, digestion, and reproductive functions. The parathyroid glands maintain the calcium level in blood and the pancreas maintains glucose homeostasis by secreting insulin and glucagon when necessary. The three gonadal steroids, androgen (testosterone), estrogen, and progesterone, regulate the development of the male and female reproductive organs.

Neurotransmitters are chemical messengers. The most common of which is acetylcholine. Acetylcholine controls muscle contraction and heartbeat. A group of neurotransmitters, the catecholamines, includes epinephrine and norepinephrine. Epinephrine (adrenaline) and norepinephrine are also hormones. They are produced in response to stress. They have profound effects on the cardiovascular and respiratory systems. These hormones/neurotransmitters can be used to increase the rate and stroke volume of the heart, thus increasing the rate of oxygen to the blood cells.

Finally, the muscular and skeletal systems are closely related. Skeletal muscles attach to the bones of the skeleton and drive movement of the body.

Skill 20.3 Analyzing physiological processes (e.g., digestion, circulation, excretion) and their role in maintaining homeostasis

Breathing and gas exchange

The respiratory system functions in the gas exchange of oxygen and carbon dioxide waste. It delivers oxygen to the bloodstream and picks up carbon dioxide for release out of the body. Air enters the mouth and nose, where it is warmed, moistened and filtered of dust and particles. Cilia in the trachea trap unwanted material in mucus, which can be expelled. The trachea splits into two bronchial tubes and the bronchial tubes divide into smaller and smaller bronchioles in the lungs. The internal surface of the lung is composed of alveoli, which are thin walled air sacs. These allow for a large surface area for gas exchange. The alveoli are lined with capillaries. Oxygen diffuses into the bloodstream and carbon dioxide diffuses out of the capillaries to be exhaled out of the lungs due to partial pressure. The oxygenated blood is carried to the heart and delivered to all parts of the body by hemoglobin, a protein consisting of iron.

The thoracic cavity holds the lungs. The diaphragm muscle below the lungs is an adaptation that makes inhalation possible. As the volume of the thoracic cavity increases, the diaphragm muscle flattens out and inhalation occurs. When the diaphragm relaxes, exhalation occurs.

Osmoregulation and waste removal

The functional unit of excretion is the nephron, which makes up the kidneys.

The structures of the excretory system and the nephron are as follows:

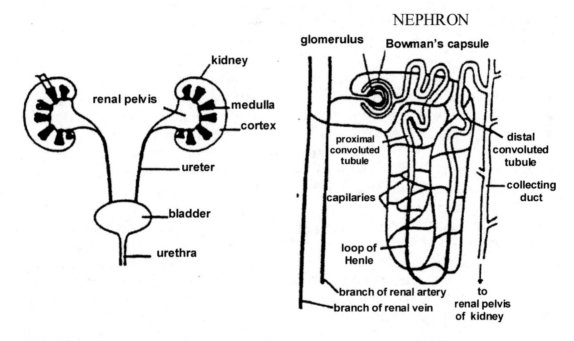

The Bowman's capsule contains the glomerulus, a tightly packed group of capillaries in the nephron. The glomerulus is under high pressure. Water, urea, salts, and other fluids leak out due to pressure into the Bowman's capsule. This fluid waste (filtrate) passes through the three regions of the nephron: the proximal convulated tubule, the loop of Henle, and the distal tubule. In the proximal convoluted tubule, unwanted molecules are secreted into the filtrate. In the loop of Henle, salt is actively pumped out of the tube and much water is lost due to the hyperosmosity of the inner part (medulla) of the kidney. As the fluid enters the distal tubule, more water is reabsorbed. Urine forms in the collecting duct that leads to the ureter then to the bladder where it is stored. Urine is passed from the bladder through the urethra. The amount of water reabsorbed back into the body is dependent upon how much water or fluids an individual has consumed. Urine can be very dilute or very concentrated if dehydration is present.

Circulatory system

There are three kinds of blood vessels in the circulatory system: arteries, capillaries, and veins. Arteries carry oxygenated blood away from the heart to organs in the body. Arteries branch off to form smaller arterioles in the organs. The arterioles form tiny capillaries that reach every tissue. At their downstream end, capillaries combine to form larger venules. Venules combine to form larger veins that return blood to the heart. Arteries and veins are distinguished by the direction in which they carry blood.

Blood vessels are lined by endothelium. In veins and arteries, the endothelium is surrounded by a layer of smooth muscle and an outer layer of elastic connective tissue. Capillaries only consist of the thin endothelium layer and its basement membrane that allows nutrients to be absorbed.

Blood flow velocity decreases as it reaches the capillaries. The capillaries have the smallest diameter of the blood vessels, but this is not why the velocity decreases. The artery conveys blood to such a large amount of capillaries that the blood flow velocity actually decelerates as it enters the capillaries. Blood pressure is the hydrostatic force that blood exerts against the wall of a vessel. Blood pressure is greater in arteries. It is the force that conveys blood from the heart through the arteries and capillaries.

Blood is a connective tissue consisting of the liquid plasma and several kinds of cells. Approximately 60% of the blood is plasma. It contains water salts called electrolytes, nutrients, waste, and proteins. The electrolytes maintain pH of about 7.4. The proteins contribute to blood viscosity and helps maintain pH. Some of the proteins are immunoglobulins are the antibodies that help fend off infection. Another group of proteins are clotting factors.

The lymphatic system is responsible for returning lost fluid and proteins to the blood. Fluid enters lymph capillaries. This lymph fluid is filtered in the lymph nodes filled with white blood cells that fight off infection.

The two classes of cells in blood are red blood cells and white blood cells. Red blood cells (erythrocytes) are the most numerous. They contain hemoglobin which carries oxygen.

White blood cells (leukocytes) are larger than red blood cells. They are phagocytic and can engulf invaders. White blood cells are not confined to the blood vessels and can enter the interstitial fluid between cells. There are five types of white blood cells: monocytes, neutophils, basophils, eosinophils, and lymphocytes.

A third cellular element found in blood is platelets. Platelets are made in the bone marrow and assist in blood clotting. The neurotransmitter that initiates blood vessel constriction following an injury is called serotonin. A material called prothrombin is converted to thrombin with the help of thromboplastin. The thrombin is then used to convert fibrinogen to fibrin, which traps red blood cells to form a scab and stop blood flow.

Nutrients and digestion

The function of the digestive system is to break food down into nutrients and absorb it into the blood stream where it can be delivered to all cells of the body for use in cellular respiration.

Essential nutrients are those nutrients that the body needs but cannot make. There are four groups of essential nutrients: essential amino acids, essential fatty acids, vitamins, and minerals.

There are about eight essential amino acids humans need. A lack of these amino acids results in protein deficiency. There are only a few essential fatty acids.

Vitamins are organic molecules essential for a nutritionally adequate diet. Thirteen vitamins essential to humans have been identified. There are two groups of vitamins: water soluble (includes the vitamin B complex and vitamin C) and water insoluble (vitamins A, D and K). Vitamin deficiencies can cause severe problems.

Unlike vitamins, minerals are inorganic molecules. Calcium is needed for bone construction and maintenance. Iron is important in cellular respiration and is a big component of hemoglobin.

Carbohydrates, fats, and proteins are fuel for the generation of ATP. Water is necessary to keep the body hydrated. The importance of water was discussed in previous sections.

Mechanical and chemical digestion

The teeth and saliva begin digestion by breaking food down into smaller pieces and lubricating it so it can be swallowed. The lips, cheeks, and tongue form a bolus or ball of food. It is carried down the pharynx by the process of peristalsis (wave-like contractions) and enters the stomach through the sphincter, which closes to keep food from going back up. In the stomach, pepsinogen and hydrochloric acid form pepsin, the enzyme that hydrolyzes proteins. The food is broken down further by this chemical action and is churned into acid chyme. The pyloric sphincter muscle opens to allow the food to enter the small intestine. Most nutrient absorption occurs in the small intestine. Its large surface area, accomplished by its length and protrusions called villi and microvilli, allow for a great absorptive surface into the bloodstream. Chyme is neutralized after coming from the acidic stomach to allow the enzymes found there to function. Accessory organs function in the production of necessary enzymes and bile. The pancreas makes many enzymes to break down food in the small intestine. The liver makes bile, which breaks down and emulsifies fatty acids. Any food left after the trip through the small intestine enters the large intestine. The large intestine functions to reabsorb water and produce vitamin K. The feces, or remaining waste, are passed out through the anus.

Skill 20.4   Demonstrating knowledge of human reproduction, growth, and development

Hormones regulate sexual maturation in humans. Humans cannot reproduce until about the puberty age of 8-14, depending on the individual. The hypothalamus begins secreting hormones that help mature the reproductive system and development of the secondary sex characteristics. Reproductive maturity in girls occurs with her first menstruation and occurs in boys with the first ejaculation of viable sperm.

Hormones also regulate reproduction. In males, the primary sex hormones are the androgens, testosterone being the most important. The androgens are produced in the testes and are responsible for the primary and secondary sex characteristics of the male. Female hormone patterns are cyclic and complex. Most women have a reproductive cycle length of about 28 days. The menstrual cycle is specific to the changes in the uterus. The ovarian cycle results in ovulation and occurs in parallel with the menstrual cycle. This parallelism is regulated by hormones. Five hormones participate in this regulation, most notably estrogen and progesterone. Estrogen and progesterone play an important role in the signaling to the uterus and the development and maintenance of the endometrium. Estrogens are also responsible for the secondary sex characteristics of females.

Gametogenesis and fertilization

Gametogenesis is the production of the sperm and egg cells. Spermatogenesis begins at puberty in the male. One spermatogonia, the diploid precursor of sperm, produces four sperm. The sperm mature in the seminiferous tubules located in the testes. Oogenesis, the production of egg cells (ova), is usually complete by the birth of a female. Egg cells are not released until menstruation begins at puberty. Meiosis forms one ovum with all the cytoplasm and three polar bodies that are reabsorbed by the body. The ovum are stored in the ovaries and released each month from puberty to menopause.

Sperm are stored in the seminiferous tubules in the testes where they mature. Mature sperm are found in the epididymis located on top of the testes. After ejaculation, the sperm travels up the vas deferens where they mix with semen made in the prostate and seminal vesicles and travel out the urethra.

Ovulation releases the egg into the fallopian tubes that are ciliated to move the egg along. Fertilization of the egg by the sperm normally occurs in the fallopian tube. If pregnancy does not occur, the egg passes through the uterus and is expelled through the vagina during menstruation. Levels of progesterone and estrogen stimulate menstruation and are affected by the implantation of a fertilized egg so menstruation will not occur.

Embryonic and fetal development

If fertilization occurs, the zygote begins dividing about 24 hours later. The resulting cells from a blastocyst and implants in about two to three days in the uterus. Implantation promotes secretion of human chorionic gonadotrophin (HCG). This is what is detected in pregnancy tests. The HCG keeps the level of progesterone elevated to maintain the uterine lining in order to feed the developing embryo until the umbilical cord forms.

Organogenesis, the development of the body organs, occurs during the first trimester of fetal development. The heart begins to beat and all the major structures are present at this time. The fetus grows very rapidly during the second trimester of pregnancy. The fetus is about 30 cm long and is very active at this stage. During the third and last trimester, fetal activity may decrease as the fetus grows. Labor is initiated by oxytocin, which causes labor contractions and dilation of the cervix. Prolactin and oxytocin cause the production of milk.

COMPETENCY 21.0 UNDERSTAND CHARACTERISTICS OF HUMAN DISEASES AND IMMUNOLOGY.

Skill 21.1 Recognizing characteristics of common human diseases, including their causes, prevention, diagnosis, and treatment

Malfunctions of the circulatory system

Cardiovascular diseases are the leading cause of death in the United States. Cardiac disease usually results in either a heart attack or a stroke. A heart attack is when cardiac muscle tissue dies, usually from coronary artery blockage. A stroke is when nervous tissue in the brain dies due to the blockage of arteries in the head.

Many heart attacks and strokes are caused by a disease called atherosclerosis. Plaques form on the inner walls of arteries, narrowing the area in which blood can flow. Arteriosclerosis is when the arteries harden from the plaque accumulation. Atherosclerosis can be prevented by a healthy diet limiting the lipids and cholesterol and exercise. High blood pressure (hypertension) promotes atherosclerosis. Diet, medication, and exercise can reduce high blood pressure and prevent atherosclerosis.

Malfunctions of the respiratory and excretory systems

Emphysema is a chronic obstructive pulmonary disease (COPD). These diseases make it difficult for a person to breathe. Airflow through the bronchial tubes is partially blocked making breathing difficult. The primary cause of emphysema is cigarette smoke. People with a deficiency in alpha$_1$-antitrypsin protein production have a greater risk of developing emphysema and at an earlier age. This protein helps protect the lungs from damage done by inflammation. This genetic deficiency is rare and can be tested for in individuals with a family history of the deficiency. There is no cure for emphysema but there are treatments available. The best prevention against emphysema is to not smoke.

Nephritis usually occurs in children. Symptoms include hypertension, decreased renal function, hematuria, and edema. Glomerulonephritis (GN) generally is a more precise term to describe this disease. Nephritis is produced by an antigen-antibody complex that causes inflammation and cell proliferation. Normal kidney tissue is damaged and if left untreated, nephritis can lead to kidney failure and death.

Malfunctions of the immune system

The immune system attacks not only microbes but cells that are not native of the host. This is the problem with skin grafts, organ transplantations, and blood transfusions. Antibodies to foreign blood and tissue types already exist in the body. If blood is transfused that is not compatible with the host, these antibodies destroy the new blood cells. There is a similar reaction when tissue and organs are transplanted.

The major histocompatibility complex (MHC) is responsible for the rejection of tissue and organ transplants. This complex is unique to each person. Cytotoxic T cells recognize the MHC on the transplanted tissue or organ as foreign and destroy these tissues. Various drugs are needed to suppress the immune system so this does not happen. The complication with this is that the patient is now more susceptible to infection.

Autoimmune disease occurs when the body's own immune system destroys its own cells. Lupus, Grave's disease, and rheumatoid arthritis are examples of autoimmune disease. There is no way to prevent autoimmune diseases. Immunodeficiency is a deficiency in either the humoral or cell mediated immune defenses. HIV is an example of an immunodeficiency disease.

Malfunctions of the digestive system

Gastric ulcers are lesions in the stomach lining. Ulcers are mainly caused by bacteria, but are worsened by pepsin and acid if the ulcers are not healed quickly enough.

Appendicitis is the inflammation of the appendix. The appendix has no known function but is open to the intestine, but can be blocked by hardened stool or swollen tissue. The blocked appendix can cause bacterial infections and inflammation leading to appendicitis. The swelling cuts the blood supply, killing the organ tissue. If left untreated, this leads to the rupture of the appendix and the stool and the infection spill out into the abdomen. This condition is life threatening if immediate surgery does not take place. Symptoms include lower abdominal pain, nausea, loss of appetite, and fever.

Malfunctions of the nervous and endocrine systems

Diabetes is the best known endocrine disorder. This is caused by a deficiency of insulin resulting in high blood glucose. Type I diabetes is an autoimmune disorder. The immune system attacks the cells of the pancreas, ending the ability to produce insulin. Treatment for type I diabetes consists of daily insulin injections. Type II diabetes usually occurs with age and/or obesity. There is usually a reduced response in target cells due to changes in insulin receptors or a deficiency of insulin. Type II diabetics need to monitor their blood glucose levels. Treatment is usually by diet and exercise.

Hyperthyroidism is another disorder of the endocrine system. This occurs from excessive secretion of thyroid hormones. Symptoms are weight loss, high blood pressure, and high body temperature. The opposite, hypothyroidism, causes weight gain, lethargy, and intolerance to cold.

There are many nervous system disorders. Parkinson's disease is caused by the degeneration of the basal ganglia in the brain. This results in the motor impulses send to the muscles to cease. Symptoms include tremors, slow movement, and muscle rigidity. Progression of Parkinson's disease occurs in five stages: early, mild, moderate, advanced, and severe. In the severe stage, the person is confined to a bed or chair. There is no cure for Parkinson's disease. Private research with stem cells is currently underway to find a cure for Parkinson's disease.

Skill 21.2   Evaluating the effects of behaviors (e.g., smoking, exercising regularly) on short- and long-term health

While genetics plays an important role in health, human behaviors can greatly affect short- and long-term health both positively and negatively. Behaviors that negatively affect health include smoking, excessive alcohol consumption, substance abuse, and poor eating habits. Behaviors that positively affect health include good nutrition and regular exercise.

Smoking negatively affects health in many ways. First, smoking decreases lung capacity, causes persistent coughing, and limits the ability to engage in strenuous physical activity. In addition, the long-term affects are even more damaging. Long-term smoking can cause lung cancer, heart disease, and emphysema (a lung disease).

Alcohol is the most abused legal drug. Excessive alcohol consumption has both short- and long-term negative effects. Drunkenness can lead to reckless behavior and distorted judgment that can cause injury or death. In addition, extreme alcohol abuse can cause alcohol poisoning that can result in immediate death. Long-term alcohol abuse is also extremely hazardous. The potential effects of long-term alcohol abuse include liver cirrhosis, heart problems, high blood pressure, stomach ulcers, and cancer.

The abuse of illegal substances can also negatively affect health. Commonly abused drugs include cocaine, heroin, opiates, methamphetamines, and marijuana. Drug abuse can cause immediate death or injury and, if used for a long time, can cause many physical and psychological health problems.

A healthy diet and regular exercise are the cornerstones of a healthy lifestyle. A diet rich in whole grains, fruits, vegetables, polyunsaturated fats, and lean protein and low in saturated fat and sugar, can positively affect overall health. Such diets can reduce cholesterol levels, lower blood pressure, and help manage body weight. Conversely, diets high in saturated fat and sugar can contribute to weight gain, heart disease, strokes, and cancer.

Finally, regular exercise has both short- and long-term health benefits. Exercise increases physical fitness, improving energy levels, overall body function, and mental well-being. Long-term, exercise helps protect against chronic diseases, maintains healthy bones and muscles, helps maintain a healthy body weight, and strengthens the body's immune system.

Skill 21.3   Demonstrating knowledge of the human immune system and the characteristics of immune responses

The immune system is responsible for defending the body against foreign invaders. There are two defense mechanisms: non specific and specific.

The non-specific immune mechanism has two lines of defenses. The first line of defense is the physical barriers of the body. These include the skin and mucous membranes. The skin prevents the penetration of bacteria and viruses as long as there are no abrasions on the skin. Mucous membranes form a protective barrier around the digestive, respiratory, and genitourinary tracts. Also, the pH of the skin and mucous membranes inhibit the growth of many microbes. Mucous secretions (tears and saliva) wash away many microbes and contain lysozyme that kills many microbes.

The second line of defense includes white blood cells and the inflammatory response. Phagocytosis is the ingestion of foreign particles. Neutrophils make up about seventy percent of all white blood cells. Monocytes mature to become macrophages which are the largest phagocytic cells. Eosinophils are also phagocytic. Natural killer cells destroy the body's own infected cells instead of the invading the microbe directly.

The other second line of defense is the inflammatory response. The blood supply to the injured area is increased, causing redness and heat. Swelling also typically occurs with inflammation. Histamine is released by basophils and mast cells when the cells are injured. This triggers the inflammatory response.

The specific immune mechanism recognizes specific foreign material and responds by destroying the invader. These mechanisms are specific and diverse. They are able to recognize individual pathogens. An antigen is any foreign particle that elicits an immune response. An antibody is manufactured by the body and recognizes and latches onto antigens, hopefully destroying them. They also have recognition of foreign material versus the self. Memory of the invaders provides immunity upon further exposure.

Immunity is the body's ability to recognize and destroy an antigen before it causes harm. Active immunity develops after recovery from an infectious disease (i.e. chicken pox) or after a vaccination (mumps, measles, rubella). Passive immunity may be passed from one individual to another and is not permanent. A good example is the immunities passed from mother to nursing child. A baby's immune system is not well developed and the passive immunity they receive through nursing keeps them healthier.

There are two main responses made by the body after exposure to an antigen:

1.   Humoral response - free antigens activate this response and B cells (a lymphocyte from bone marrow) give rise to plasma cells that secrete antibodies and memory cells that will recognize future exposures to the same antigen. The antibodies defend against extracellular pathogens by binding to the antigen and making them an easy target for phagocytes to engulf and destroy. Antibodies are in a class of proteins called immunoglobulins. There are five major classes of immunoglobulins (Ig) involved in the humoral response: IgM, IgG, IgA, IgD, and IgE.

2.   Cell mediated response - cells that have been infected activate T cells (a lymphocyte from the thymus). These activated T cells defend against pathogens in the cells or cancer cells by binding to the infected cell and destroying them along with the antigen. T cell receptors on the T helper cells recognize antigens bound to the body's own cells. T helper cells release IL-2 which stimulates other lymphocytes (cytotoxic T cells and B cells). Cytotoxic T cells kill infected host cells by recognizing specific antigens.

Vaccines are antigens given in very small amounts. They stimulate both humoral and cell mediated responses and memory cells recognize future exposure to the antigen so antibodies can be produced much faster.

COMPETENCY 22.0 UNDERSTAND THE CHARACTERISTICS OF POPULATIONS AND COMMUNITIES.

Skill 22.1   Identifying the basic requirements of organisms (e.g., nutrients, space)

All organisms are adapted to life in their unique habitat. The habitat includes all the components of their physical environment and is a necessity for the species' survival. Below are several key components of a complete habitat that all organisms require.

Food and water

Because all biochemical reactions take place in aqueous environments, all organisms must have access to clean water, even if only infrequently. Organisms also require two types of food: a source of energy (fixed carbon) and a source of nutrients. Autotrophs can fix carbon for themselves, but must have access to certain inorganic precursors. These organisms must also be able to obtain other nutrients, such as nitrogen, from their environment. Hetertrophs, on the other hand, must consume other organisms for both energy and nutrients. The species these organisms use as a food source must be present in their habitat.

Sunlight and air

This need is closely related to that for food and water because almost all species derive some needed nutrients from the sun and atmosphere. Plants require carbon dioxide to photosynthesize and oxygen is required for cellular respiration. Sunlight is also necessary for photosynthesis and is used by many animals to synthesize essential nutrients (i.e. vitamin D).

Shelter and space

The need for shelter and space vary greatly between species. Many plants do not need shelter, per se, but must have adequate soil to spread their roots and acquire nutrients. Certain invasive species can threaten native plants by out-competing them for space. Other types of plants and many animals also require protection from environmental hazards. These locations may facilitate reproduction (for instance, nesting sites) or provide seasonal shelter (for examples, dens and caves used by hibernating species).

Skill 22.2   Demonstrating knowledge of the concept of an ecological niche

The term 'Niche' describes the relational position of a species or population in an ecosystem. Niche includes how a population responds to the abundance of its resources and enemies (e.g., by growing when resources are abundant and predators, parasites and pathogens are scarce).

Niche also indicates the life history of an organism, habitat and place in the food chain. According to the competitive exclusion principle, no two species can occupy the same niche in the same environment for a long time. The full range of environmental conditions (biological and physical) under which an organism can exist describes its fundamental niche. Because of the pressure from superior competitors, superior are driven to occupy a niche much narrower than their previous niche. This is known as the 'realized niche.' Examples of niche:

1. Oak trees:
* live in forests
* absorb sunlight by photosynthesis
* provide shelter for many animals
* act as support for creeping plants
* serve as a source of food for animals
* cover their ground with dead leaves in the autumn

If the oak trees were cut down or destroyed by fire or storms they would no longer be doing their job and this would have a disastrous effect on all the other organisms living in the same habitat.

2. Hedgehogs:
* eat a variety of insects and other invertebrates which live underneath the dead leaves and twigs in the garden
* the spines are a superb environment for fleas and ticks
* put the nitrogen back into the soil when they urinate
* eat slugs and protect plants from them

If there were no hedgehogs around, the population of slugs would explode and the nutrients in the dead leaves and twigs will not be recycled.
The idea of an ecological niche is very simple. You just need to know where the animal or plant lives and what it does.

Skill 22.3 Evaluating conditions that affect population size and growth rate (e.g., birth rate, limiting factors)

A population is a group of individuals of one species that live in the same general area. Many factors can affect the population size and its growth rate. Population size can depend on the total amount of life a habitat can support. This is the carrying capacity of the environment. Once the habitat runs out of food, water, shelter, or space, the carrying capacity decreases, and then stabilizes.

Limiting factors can affect population growth. As a population increases, the competition for resources is more intense, and the growth rate declines. This is a density-dependent growth factor. The carrying capacity can be determined by the density-dependent factor. Density-independent factors affect the individuals regardless of population size. The weather and climate are good examples. Too hot or too cold temperatures may kill many individuals from a population that has not reached its carrying capacity.

Zero population growth rate occurs when the birth and death rates are equal in a population. Exponential growth rate occurs when there is and abundance of resources and the growth rate is at its maximum, called the intrinsic rate of increase. This relationship can be understood in a growth curve.

An exponentially growing population starts off with a little change, then rapidly increases.

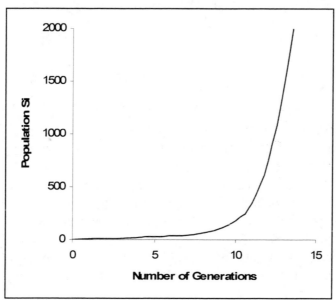

Logistic population growth incorporates the carrying capacity into the growth rate. As a population reaches the carrying capacity, the growth rate begins to slow down and level off.

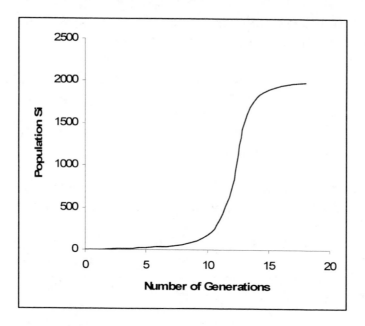

Many populations follow this model of population growth. Humans, however, are an exponentially growing population. Eventually, the carrying capacity of the Earth will be reached, and the growth rate will level off. How and when this will occur remains a mystery.

Skill 22.4 Analyzing the interrelationships among organisms in a community (e.g., predator/prey, symbiosis)

There are many interactions that may occur between different species living together. Predation, parasitism, competition, commensalisms, and mutualism are the different types of relationships populations have amongst each other.

Predation and parasitism result in a benefit for one species and a detriment for the other. Predation is when a predator eats its prey. The common conception of predation is of a carnivore consuming other animals. This is one form of predation. Although not always resulting in the death of the plant, herbivory is a form of predation. Some animals eat enough of a plant to cause death. Parasitism involves a predator that lives on or in their hosts, causing detrimental effects to the host. Insects and viruses living off and reproducing in their hosts is an example of parasitism. Many plants and animals have defenses against predators. Some plants have poisonous chemicals that will harm the predator if ingested and some animals are camouflaged so they are harder to detect.

Competition is when two or more species in a community use the same resources. Competition is usually detrimental to both populations. Competition is often difficult to find in nature because competition between two populations is not continuous. Either the weaker population will no longer exist, or one population will evolve to utilize other available resources.

Symbiosis is when two species live close together. Parasitism is one example of symbiosis described above. Another example of symbiosis is commensalisms. Commensalism occurs when one species benefits from the other without harmful effects. Mutualism is when both species benefit from the other. Species involved in mutualistic relationships must coevolve to survive. As one species evolves, the other must as well if it is to be successful in life. The grouper and a species of shrimp live in a mutualistic relationship. The shrimp feed off parasites living on the grouper; thus the shrimp are fed and the grouper stays healthy. Many microorganisms are in mutualistic relationships.

Skill 22.5   Recognizing patterns and processes of ecological succession

Succession is an orderly process of replacing a community that has been damaged or has begun where no life previously existed. Primary succession occurs where life never existed before, as in a flooded area or a new volcanic island. Secondary succession takes place in communities that were once flourishing but disturbed by some source, either man or nature, but not totally stripped. A climax community is a community that is established and flourishing.

Abiotic and biotic factors play a role in succession. Biotic factors are living things in an ecosystem; plants, animals, bacteria, fungi, etc. Abiotic factors are non-living aspects of an ecosystem; soil quality, rainfall, temperature, etc.

Abiotic factors affect succession by way of the species that colonize the area. Certain species will or will not survive depending on the weather, climate, or soil makeup. Biotic factors such as inhibition of one species due to another may occur. This may be due to some form of competition between the species.

COMPETENCY 23.0 UNDERSTAND FACTORS THAT INFLUENCE HUMAN POPULATION GROWTH AND DIVERSITY.

Skill 23.1 Recognizing characteristics and consequences of human population growth

The human population has been growing exponentially for centuries. People are living longer and healthier lives than ever before. Better health care and nutrition practices have helped in the survival of the population.

Human activity affects parts of the nutrient cycles by removing nutrients from one part of the biosphere and adding them to another. This results in nutrient depletion in one area and nutrient excess in another. This affects water systems, crops, wildlife, and humans.

Humans are responsible for the depletion of the ozone layer. This depletion is due to chemicals used for refrigeration and aerosols. The consequences of ozone depletion will be severe. Ozone protects the Earth from the majority of UV radiation. An increase of UV will promote skin cancer and unknown effects on wildlife and plants.

Skill 23.2 Relating historical patterns of human population growth to changing patterns of resource use and availability

Human population increased slowly until 1650. Since 1650, the human population has grown almost exponentially, reaching its current population of over 6 billion. Factors that have led to this increased growth rate include improved nutrition, sanitation, and health care. In addition, advances in technology, agriculture, and scientific knowledge have made the use of resources more efficient and increased their availability.

While the Earth's ultimate carrying capacity for humans is uncertain, some factors that may limit growth are the availability of food, water, space, and fossil fuels. There is a finite amount of land on Earth available for food production. In addition, providing clean, potable water for a growing human population is a real concern. Finally, fossil fuels, important energy sources for human technology, are scarce. The inevitable shortage of energy in the Earth's future will require the development of alternative energy sources to maintain or increase human population growth.

Skill 23.3   Recognizing factors that contribute to human diversity (e.g., adaptations to different environments)

Theories on the origin of human diversity fall along the continuum between neutralist and selectionist. Neutralists argue that variations in the human population, beginning with mutations at the molecular level, are random and rarely favorable. Thus, changes in genetic make-up depend on random genetic drift and mutation rate, not natural selection of favorable traits. Selectionists, on the other hand, argue that genetic polymorphisms result from adaptations to environmental conditions. Thus, while polymorphisms may impart no identifiable advantage, randomness cannot adequately explain the frequency of such traits.

Adaptation to different environments is the main theory advanced by selectionists to explain human diversity. A classic example of environmental adaptation is the advantage of sickle-cell anemia heterozygotes in resisting malarial parasites. Because heterozygotes are better able to survive malarial infections, the damaging sickle-cell trait persists in tropical environments. Another example is the advantage of individuals that are heterozygotic for the recessive disease Cystic Fibrosis in resisting typhoid fever. Finally, also supporting the selectionist theory of human diversity is the congenital increased lung capacity and cardiovascular function of high altitude populations.

From the available evidence, it is safe to assume that random variation and environmental adaptation both play a strong role in the development of human diversity.

COMPETENCY 24.0 ANALYZE THE TRANSFER OF ENERGY IN ECOSYSTEMS.

Skill 24.1 Identifying the ultimate source of energy for various types of ecosystems

The ultimate source of energy for most ecosystems is solar radiation. Primary producers are usually the organisms in an ecosystem that can convert light energy into chemical energy. Most primary producers are photosynthetic. Photosynthetic primary producers include algae, plants, and many species of bacteria. All other organisms in an ecosystem depend on primary producers to provide energy.

The main primary producers in terrestrial ecosystems are plants. In limnetic (deep-water) zone lake and pond ecosystems and open ocean ecosystems, algae and photosynthetic bacteria are the most important primary producers. In littoral (shallow water, near-shore) zone freshwater and ocean ecosystems, the main primary producers are aquatic plants and multicellular algae. Finally, one notable exception to the photosynthetic organism as primary producer rule are ecosystems near hot water vents on the deep-sea floor. Because solar energy is unavailable, chemoautotrophic bacteria that can oxidize hydrogen sulfide are the primary producers.

Skill 24.2 Analyzing the flow of energy through the trophic levels of an ecosystem

Trophic levels are based on the feeding relationships that determine energy flow and chemical cycling.

Autotrophs are the primary producers of the ecosystem. Producers mainly consist of plants. Primary consumers are the next trophic level. The primary consumers are the herbivores that eat plants or algae. Secondary consumers are the carnivores that eat the primary consumers. Tertiary consumers eat the secondary consumer. These trophic levels may go higher depending on the ecosystem. Decomposers are consumers that feed off animal waste and dead organisms. This pathway of food transfer is known as the food chain.

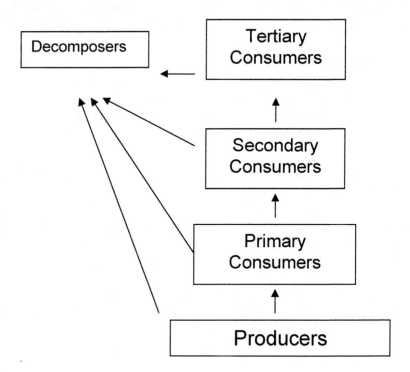

Most food chains are more elaborate, becoming food webs.

Skill 24.3   Demonstrating knowledge of factors that affect ecosystem productivity and the efficiency with which energy is transferred from one level to the next

Several environmental factors affect ecosystem productivity and the rate and efficiency of consumption affects the efficiency of energy transfer between trophic levels.

Primary producers convert solar energy into chemical energy through photosynthesis. The factors most important in limiting ecosystem productivity are light intensity, temperature, and precipitation. As light intensity increases, ecosystem productivity increases. Thus, terrestrial ecosystems closer to the equator and aquatic ecosystems closer to the water's surface are more productive than polar ecosystems and deep-water ecosystems. Extreme temperatures also limit ecosystem productivity. In general, cold temperatures limit productivity in ecosystems distant from the equator. Finally, lack of precipitation can limit productivity. Primary producers require adequate levels of water to achieve high levels of productivity. Thus, deserts and tundra ecosystems have low productivity.

As energy flows through an ecosystem, much of it is lost before consumers can use it. For example, herbivores do not eat all of the plant structures in an ecosystem and they cannot digest all of the plant material they do eat. In addition, consumers do not use all of the energy consumed for growth. Much of the consumed energy is lost to the environment as heat during respiration. Because eating plant products directly, rather than eating meat, is the most efficient means of energy transfer, ecosystems dominated by herbivores are generally more efficient than ecosystems dominated by carnivores.

Skill 24.4   Comparing energy, numbers, and biomass pyramids for different types of ecosystems

Energy is lost as the trophic levels progress from producer to tertiary consumer. The amount of energy that is transferred between trophic levels is called the ecological efficiency. The visual of this energy flow is represented in a pyramid of productivity.

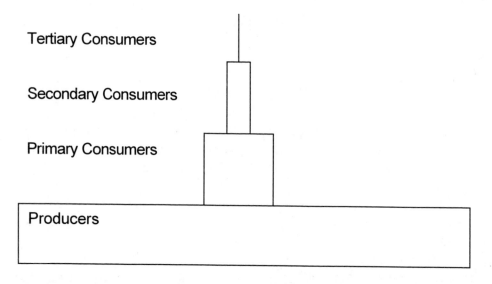

The biomass pyramid represents the total dry weight of organisms in each trophic level. A pyramid of numbers is a representation of the population size of each trophic level. The producers, being the most populous, are on the bottom of this pyramid with the tertiary consumers on the top with the fewest numbers.

COMPETENCY 25.0 UNDERSTAND BIOGEOCHEMICAL CYCLES.

Skill 25.1   Recognizing characteristics and processes of biogeochemical cycles (e.g., water, carbon, nitrogen)

Biogeochemical cycles are nutrient cycles that involve both biotic and abiotic factors.

Water cycle - 2% of all the available water is fixed and unavailable in ice or the bodies of organisms. Available water includes surface water (lakes, ocean, rivers) and ground water (aquifers, wells) 96% of all available water is from ground water. The water cycle is driven by solar energy. Water is recycled through the processes of evaporation and precipitation. The water present now is the water that has been here since our atmosphere formed.

Carbon cycle - Ten percent of all available carbon in the air (from carbon dioxide gas) is fixed by photosynthesis. Plants fix carbon in the form of glucose, animals eat the plants and are able to obtain their source of carbon. When animals release carbon dioxide through respiration, the plants again have a source of carbon to fix again.

Nitrogen cycle - Eighty percent of the atmosphere is in the form of nitrogen gas. Nitrogen must be fixed and taken out of the gaseous form to be incorporated into an organism. Only a few genera of bacteria have the correct enzymes to break the triple bond between nitrogen atoms in a process called nitrogen fixation. These bacteria live within the roots of legumes (peas, beans, alfalfa) and add nitrogen to the soil so it may be taken up by the plant. Nitrogen is necessary to make amino acids and the nitrogenous bases of DNA.

Phosphorus cycle - Phosphorus exists as a mineral and is not found in the atmosphere. Fungi and plant roots have a structure called mycorrhizae that are able to fix insoluble phosphates into useable phosphorus. Urine and decayed matter return phosphorus to the earth where it can be fixed in the plant. Phosphorus is needed for the backbone of DNA and for ATP manufacturing.

Skill 25.2   Demonstrating knowledge of the roles of decomposers, producers, and consumers in the cycling of nutrients

Autotrophs are the primary producers of the ecosystem. Producers mainly consist of plants. Primary consumers are the next trophic level. The primary consumers are the herbivores that eat plants or algae. Secondary consumers are the carnivores that eat the primary consumers. Tertiary consumers eat the secondary consumer. These trophic levels may go higher depending on the ecosystem. Decomposers are consumers that feed off animal waste and dead organisms. In the carbon cycle, decomposers recycle the carbon accumulated in durable organic material that do not immediately proceed to the carbon cycle. Ammonification is the decomposition of organic nitrogen back to ammonia.

This process in the nitrogen cycle is carried out by aerobic and anaerobic bacterial and fungal decomposers. Decomposers add phosphorous back to the soil by decomposing the excretion of animals.

Skill 25.3 Evaluating factors that affect the release and cycling of nutrients

A limiting factor is the component of a biological process that determines how quickly or slowly the process proceeds. Photosynthesis is the main biological process determining the rate of ecosystem productivity, the rate at which an ecosystem creates biomass. Thus, in evaluating the productivity of an ecosystem, potential limiting factors are light intensity, gas concentrations, and mineral availability. The Law of the Minimum states that the required factor in a given process that is most scarce controls the rate of the process.

One potential limiting factor of ecosystem productivity is light intensity because photosynthesis requires light energy. Light intensity can limit productivity in two ways. First, too little light limits the rate of photosynthesis because the required energy is not available. Second, too much light can damage the photosynthetic system of plants and microorganisms thus slowing the rate of photosynthesis. Decreased photosynthesis equals decreased productivity.

Another potential limiting factor of ecosystem productivity is gas concentrations. Photosynthesis requires carbon dioxide. Thus, increased concentration of carbon dioxide often results in increased productivity. While carbon dioxide is often not the ultimate limiting factor of productivity, increased concentration can indirectly increase rates of photosynthesis in several ways. First, increased carbon dioxide concentration often increases the rate of nitrogen fixation (available nitrogen is another limiting factor of productivity). Second, increased carbon dioxide concentration can decrease the pH of rain, improving the water source of photosynthetic organisms.

Finally, mineral availability also limits ecosystem productivity. Plants require adequate amounts of nitrogen and phosphorus to build many cellular structures. The availability of the inorganic minerals phosphorus and nitrogen often is the main limiting factor of plant biomass production. In other words, in a natural environment phosphorus and nitrogen availability most often limits ecosystem productivity, rather than carbon dioxide concentration or light intensity.

COMPETENCY 26.0 ANALYZE THE EFFECTS OF NATURAL PHENOMENA AND HUMAN ACTIVITIES ON ECOSYSTEMS.

Skill 26.1   Identifying the effects of natural phenomena on ecosystems (e.g., volcanic eruptions, floods)

Natural phenomena affect the make up and functioning of ecosystems both directly and indirectly. For example, floods and volcanic eruptions can destroy the fixed portions of an ecosystem, such as plants and microbes. Mobile elements, such as animals, must evacuate or risk injury or death. After a catastrophic event, species of microbes and plants begin to repopulate the ecosystem, beginning a line of secondary succession that eventually leads to the return of higher-level species. Often the area affected by the event returns to something like its original state.

Volcanic eruptions produce large amounts of molten lava and expel large amounts of ash and gas. Molten lava kills and destroys any living organisms it contacts. However, when lava cools and hardens, it provides a rich environment for growth of microbes and plants. Volcanic eruptions also affect ecosystems indirectly. Studies show that the ash and gas released by eruptions can cause a reduction in the area temperature for several years. The volcanic aerosol reflects the Sun's rays and creates clouds that have the same effect. In addition, sulfuric acid released by the volcano suppresses the production of greenhouse gases that damage the ozone layer.

Floods destroy microbes and vegetation and kill or force the evacuation of animals. Only when floodwaters recede can an ecosystem begin to return to normal. Floods, however, also have indirect effects. For example, floods can cause permanent soil erosion and nutrient depletion. Such disruptions of the soil can delay and limit an ecosystem's recovery.

Skill 26.2   Identifying types, sources, and effects of pollution

Pollution includes environmental contamination by chemical, physical, biological, and radioactive substances. Major types of pollution include:

Air pollution- The release of a variety of chemicals and particulates causes air pollution. These include carbon monoxide, sulfur dioxide and chlorofluorocarbons (CFC's) as well as carbon particulates. The release of compounds derived from sulfur and nitrogen impurities in fossil fuels contribute to air pollution. Smog is a particular type of air pollution caused by a reaction between sunlight and compounds such as nitrogen oxide and volatile organic compounds which leads to the brown haze over large cities.

Water pollution- Contaminants enter the water system either by ground runoff or by leaching. Historically, industrial waste was dumped directly into bodies of water, but this is more regulated now. However, agricultural runoff continues to pollute water supplies. Buried waste, such as that in landfills, may also leach harmful substances into the soil and groundwater.

Thermal pollution- While industrial facilities typically no longer dispose of contaminants into bodies of water, they may dump water at high temperatures back into the environment. The very hot water both increases temperatures above normal and decreases the concentration of dissolved gases, since gases are less soluble in warm water. Both these effects are disruptive to the local ecosystem.

Radioactive contamination- Radioactive waste from medical, research, and power plant facilities has not always been carefully handled. Accidental leakage and failure to adequately contain waste has led to radioactive pollution in both water and soil.

In addition to certain processes releasing these contaminants into the environment, there are secondary effects in many cases. For instance, many harmful effects have resulted from the combustion of fossil fuels to produce energy for industrial, commercial, and residential facilities as well as to power many types of automobiles. If pure hydrocarbons are burned in oxygen, the only products of combustion are carbon dioxide and water. However, combustion is typically done in air so nitrogen is also present during the reaction resulting in the formation of nitrous oxides. Impurities in the fuel itself mean that compounds such as sulfur dioxide are also formed during combustion. Finally, incomplete combustion releases carbon monoxide. The following are a few of the known detrimental effects of fossil fuel combustion:

Greenhouse gases- While many "greenhouse gases" such as carbon dioxide and nitrous oxide are naturally occurring, their concentration in the atmosphere has dramatically increased as result of fossil fuel use. Greenhouse gases absorb and trap heat, thus warming the planet and possibly triggering climate change.

Acid rain- Sulfur and nitrous oxides are converted to sulfuric and nitric acid in rain. At sufficient concentrations, they will significantly lower the pH of the rain. This acid rain damages man-made and natural structures. Worse yet, it contaminates our planet's water supplies, damaging not only lakes and rivers and their ecosystems but also groundwater and forests.

Skill 26.3 Analyzing the consequences of human activities, such as habitat destruction, introduction of exotic species, and burning of fossil fuels, on the environment and species diversity

Deforestation for urban development has resulted in the extinction or relocation of several species of plants and animals. Animals are forced to leave their forest homes or perish amongst the destruction. The number of plant and animal species that have become extinct due to deforestation is unknown. Scientists have only identified a fraction of the species on Earth. It is known that if the destruction of natural resources continues, there may be no plants or animals successfully reproducing in the wild.

The following are some of the detrimental results of our improper use of space:

-Fertilizer run-off has led to excess nitrogen and phosphorus in rivers and lakes; ammonia in the fertilizer often gases off and contributes to air pollution
-Excess herbicides, insecticides and other such chemicals have harmed the native species
-Soil has eroded from intense tillage
-Biodiversity has been lost as ecosystems are destroyed and much land is dedicated to the production of only a few crops (corn, rice, wheat, etc.)
-Minerals and organic compounds to which the soil owed its natural fertility have been lost

Sustainable agriculture methods aim to keep farmland producing perpetually. These approaches must maintain the fertility of the soil without causing detrimental environment effects. Unfortunately, few such methods are currently in use on a large scale. Thus, while they are highly promising, it has been difficult to demonstrate their economic viability or ability to produce large amounts of food.

Skill 26.4 Evaluating the effectiveness of methods and technologies designed to reduce or mitigate environmental damage

Environmental degradation is damage to an ecosystem, or the biosphere as a whole, resulting from human activities. The underlying causes of environmental degradation are production of energy and consumer products, human population growth and development, and waste disposal. Production of energy and consumer products pollutes the air and contributes to global warming. In addition, harvesting of natural resources can deplete supplies and damage ecosystems. Growth and development of human communities can diminish natural resource supplies, damage the land, and disrupt natural ecosystems. Finally, improper waste disposal can pollute the land and water supplies.

Scientists and policy makers continually attempt to develop and implement new methods and technologies to reduce or mitigate environmental degradation. Cleaner burning fuels or alternative sources of energy that do not pollute the air potential solutions to the energy production-air pollution trade off. In addition, the treatment and filtering of fuel burning by-products can limit environmental impact. However, both developing alternative energy sources and treating current emissions are costly processes. In a market driven economy, governments and policy makers must provide incentives and implement regulations to encourage and require environmental responsibility.

Growth and development of human communities, while inevitable, requires careful planning and attention to environmental concerns. Governmental regulations are often necessary to limit the affect of growth on surrounding ecosystems. Developers and policy makers must attempt to balance the need for increased housing and construction with the importance of respecting and maintaining biodiversity and ecosystem function.

Finally, improper waste disposal can pollute the land and water. Many human and industrial waste products are highly toxic and can cause irreversible environmental damage. Methods of reducing environmental degradation resulting from waste disposal include careful treatment of sewage and human waste, safe disposal of waste products in properly designed locations, and recycling and reuse of waste products.

COMPETENCY 27.0 UNDERSTAND RESOURCE USE AND MANAGEMENT BY HUMANS.

Skill 27.1   Identifying types of resources used by humans (e.g., mineral, plant, fossil fuels)

Humans have a tremendous impact on the world's natural resources. The world's natural water supplies are affected by human use. Waterways are major sources for recreation and freight transportation. Oil and wastes from boats and cargo ships pollute the aquatic environment. The aquatic plant and animal life is affected by this contamination. To obtain drinking water, contaminants such as parasites, pollutants and bacteria are removed from raw water through a purification process involving various screening, conditioning and chlorination steps. Most uses of water resources, such as drinking and crop irrigation, require fresh water. Only 2.5% of water on Earth is fresh water, and more than two thirds of this fresh water is frozen in glaciers and polar ice caps. Consequently, in many parts of the world, water use greatly exceeds supply. This problem is expected to increase in the future.

Plant resources also make up a large part of the world's natural resources. Plant resources are renewable and can be re-grown and restocked. Plant resources can be used by humans to make clothing, buildings and medicines, and can also be directly consumed. Forestry is the study and management of growing forests. This industry provides the wood that is essential for use as construction timber or paper. Cotton is a common plant found on farms of the Southern United States. Cotton is used to produce fabric for clothing, sheets, furniture, etc. Another example of a plant resource that is not directly consumed is straw, which is harvested for use in plant growth and farm animal care. The list of plants grown to provide food for the people of the world is extensive. Major crops include corn, potatoes, wheat, sugar, barley, peas, beans, beets, flax, lentils, sunflowers, soybeans, canola, and rice. These crops may have alternate uses as well. For example, corn is used to manufacture cornstarch, ethanol fuel, high fructose corn syrup, ink, biodegradable plastics, chemicals used in cosmetics and pharmaceuticals, adhesives, and paper products.

Other resources used by humans are known as "non-renewable" resources. Such resources, including fossil fuels, cannot be re-made and do not naturally reform at a rate that could sustain human use. Non-renewable resources are therefore depleted and not restored. Presently, non-renewable resources provide the main source of energy for humans. Common fossil fuels used by humans are coal, petroleum and natural gas, which all form from the remains of dead plants and animals through natural processes after millions of years. Because of their high carbon content, when burnt these substances generate high amounts of energy as well as carbon dioxide, which is released back into the atmosphere increasing global warming. To create electricity, energy from the burning of fossil fuels is harnessed to power a rotary engine called a turbine.

Implementation of the use of fossil fuels as an energy source provided for large-scale industrial development.

Mineral resources are concentrations of naturally occurring inorganic elements and compounds located in the Earth's crust that are extracted through mining for human use. Minerals have a definite chemical composition and are stable over a range of temperatures and pressures. Construction and manufacturing rely heavily on metals and industrial mineral resources. These metals may include iron, bronze, lead, zinc, nickel, copper, tin, etc. Other industrial minerals are divided into two categories: bulk rocks and ore minerals. Bulk rocks, including limestone, clay, shale and sandstone, are used as aggregate in construction, in ceramics or in concrete. Common ore minerals include calcite, barite and gypsum. Energy from some minerals can be utilized to produce electricity fuel and industrial materials. Mineral resources are also used as fertilizers and pesticides in the industrial context.

Skill 27.2   Recognizing the role of technology in obtaining and managing resources

Technology has been instrumental in helping us to curb pollution and improve the quality of resources. Some of the most common areas are wastewater treatment, recycling, and food safety.

Waste water treatment

Wastewater treatment is the process by which contaminants are removed from sewage. In addition to physical and chemical processing, biological methods are used to clean the wastewater and make it suitable for release back into the environment. Indigenous bacteria can be used to remove biological matter dissolved in the water. Activated sludge is the process in which sewage is aerated to allow the growth of various organisms, collectively known as biological floc, including saprophytic bacteria and protozoan. Advances in biotechnology have led to better management of activated sludge, allowing it to remove the bulk of organic material and the conversion of ammonia to nitrogen gas. These advances include moving bed biological reactors, biological aerated filters, and membrane biological reactors.

Contaminant Reduction

Various technologies have been invented to reduce the amount of contaminants released. The devices typically use filters to trap the pollutants or rely on chemical reactions to neutralize them. Examples of the former include electrostatic air cleaners and fabric air filters. Examples of the latter include catalytic converters and scrubbers. Materials such as activated charcoal have properties of both types, since they trap and partially neutralize many contaminants, but may still require further chemical treatment. Another key area in which technological advances may be help control pollution is in the search for alternative fuels. Possible alternative energy sources include biodiesel, nuclear power, biomethanol, hydrogen fuel, and fuel cells. Increasing the efficiency of solar fuel cells, hydroelectricity, and wind energy may also help reduce dependence on fossil fuels.

Recycling

Additionally, recycling programs for a variety of materials have begun. Recycling is the reprocessing of materials into new products. Recycling prevents many materials from becoming waste and also avoids the need to harvest new materials. For many materials, recycling requires less energy than virgin production. The most commonly recycled materials are glass, paper, aluminum, asphalt, steel, textiles, and plastic. Recycling can occur either pre-consumer or post-consumer.

Food safety

Food borne illness is caused by the consumption of food contaminated with pathogenic bacteria, viruses, parasites, or other biological toxins. The best preventative measure is still proper controls and hygiene during food preparation. However, advances in biotechnology now mean that screening of food for toxins and pathogens can be done more easily. For instance, a fluorescent optical biosensor is currently being developed to measure antibiotic contaminants in milk. The biosensor measures reactions taking place on an antibody-coated probe in contact with the milk products. As testing becomes faster and cheaper, a larger percentage of the food we eat can be screened. Better biological testing methods may also help us identify pathogens that are currently unknown; the cause of approximately 60% of food borne illness is still not known.

Skill 27.3   Analyzing issues related to the availability, distribution, and use of resources

The Earth has a finite supply of fresh water located in aquifers, surface water, and the atmosphere. Not only does this finite supply tend to make water scarce in some regions, but also many water supplies are now undrinkable due to water pollution. Overpopulation in many areas has exacerbated these shortages. Because ground and surface water is being overused, times of drought are also especially devastating. Issues with the water supply have led to many problems for human beings and all living things; a few are listed below:

-Over 1 billion people have inadequate access to safe drinking water and over 2 billion do not have enough water for safe sanitation
-The use of diseased or polluted water is thought to be responsible for up to 80% of human illness
-Overuse and pollution of existing supplies has damaged many ecosystems and resulted in declining biodiversity
-Lack of water and lowering of water tables has decreased agricultural yields
-Political strife in dry areas often results from disputes over water availability

Water shortages are particularly difficult to handle because few technological solutions are possible. Those that exist, such as desalination of seawater, are prohibitively expensive for most countries. More sustainable solutions must be found to guarantee the success of agriculture, continued biodiversity, and the future of the human race.

Space

Not simply space, but tillable land capable of producing food has become scarcer as the earth's population has increased. To meet the food demands of an ever growing population, many forests have been cut down and wetlands have been drained to produce more farming fields. This has been detrimental to biodiversity. Additionally, tropical deforestation has damaged the entire earth's ecosystem, since these forests produce much of the planet's oxygen. In other areas, fertile farmland has been converted to residential and industrial space. As a result, farming has also become increasing intensive; large amounts of chemicals have been applied to land of decreasing fertility in attempt to grow more food in smaller areas.

Energy

The current energy crisis is largely centered on the uncertain future of fossil fuels. The supplies of fossil fuels are limited and fast declining. Additionally, most oil is now derived from a highly politically volatile area of the world. Finally, continuing to produce energy from fossils fuels is unwise given the damage done by both the disruption to the environment necessary to harvest them and the byproducts of their combustion cause pollution.

It is important to recognize that a real energy crisis has vast economic implications. Oil, currently the most important fossil fuel, is needed for heating, electricity, and as a raw material for the manufacture of many items, particularly plastics. Additionally, the gasoline made from oil is important in transporting people and goods, including food and other items necessary for life. A disruption in the oil supply often causes rising prices in all sectors and may eventually trigger recession.

Skill 27.4 Recognizing strategies used to manage various types of resources

As the detrimental effects of pollution have received increasing attention, a number of legislative initiatives have been undertaken to control the pollution and mitigate its effect. The US Environmental Protection Agency (EPA) was established in 1970 to protect human health by reducing damage to the environment. They continue to define and enforce standards for pollution control. The Clean Air (1963) and Clean Water (1977) Acts were two major milestones in the legal control of pollutants.

Finally, many groups now exist to advocate for either conservation or preservation of natural resources. Preservationists are in favor of the strict setting aside of land from human use. Conservationists, on the other hand, prefer sustainable development of land. Preserves are not subjected to any human involvement and so unhealthy overpopulation of a single species is a common problem. Conservation areas or refuges are more actively managed and so typically have more biodiversity. Conservation initiatives are responsible for saving both species and habitats by protecting them from detrimental human involvement.

Sample Test

Directions: Read each item and select the best response.

1. **A student designed a science project testing the effects of light and water on plant growth. You would recommend that she**

   A. manipulate the temperature as well.

   B. also alter the pH of the water as another variable.

   C. omit either water or light as a variable.

   D. also alter the light concentration as another variable.

2. **Identify the control in the following experiment. A student had four plants grown under the following conditions and was measuring photosynthetic rate by measuring mass: 2 plants in 50% light and 2 plants in 100% light.**

   A. plants grown with no added nutrients

   B. plants grown in the dark

   C. plants in 100% light

   D. plants in 50% light

3. **In an experiment measuring the growth of bacteria at different temperatures, identify the independent variable.**

   A. growth of number of colonies

   B. temperature

   C. type of bacteria used

   D. light intensity

4. **A scientific theory**

   A. proves scientific accuracy.
   B. is never rejected.
   C. results in a medical breakthrough.
   D. may be altered at a later time.

5. **Which is the correct order of methodology? 1) testing revised explanation, 2) setting up a controlled experiment to test explanation, 3) drawing a conclusion, 4) suggesting an explanation for observations, and 5) compare observed results to hypothesized results**

   A. 4, 2, 3, 1, 5

   B. 3, 1, 4, 2, 5

   C. 4, 2, 5, 1, 3

   D. 2, 5, 4, 1, 3

6. **Given a choice, which is the most desirable method of heating a substance in the lab?**

   A. alcohol burner

   B. gas burner

   C. bunsen burner

   D. hot plate

7. **Biological waste should be disposed of**

   A. in the trash can.

   B. under a fume hood.

   C. in the broken glass box.

   D. in an autoclavable biohazard bag.

8. **Chemicals should be stored**

   A. in a cool dark room.

   B. in a dark room.

   C. according to their reactivity with other substances.

   D. in a double locked room.

9. **Given the choice of lab activities, which would you omit?**

   A. a genetics experiment tracking the fur color of mice

   B. dissecting a preserved fetal pig

   C. a lab relating temperature to respiration rate using live goldfish.

   D. pithing a frog to see the action of circulation

10. **Who should be notified in the case of a serious chemical spill?**

    I. the custodian
    II. The fire department
    III. the chemistry teacher
    IV. the administration

    A. I

    B. II

    C. II and III

    D. II and IV

11. **The "Right to Know" law states:**

    A. the inventory of toxic chemicals checked against the "Substance List" be available.

    B. that students are to be informed on alternatives to dissection.

    C. that science teachers are to be informed of student allergies.

    D. that students are to be informed of infectious microorganisms used in lab.

12. **In which situation would a science teacher be liable?**

A. a teacher leaves to receive an emergency phone call and a student slips and falls.

B. a student removes their goggles and gets dissection fluid in their eye.

C. a faulty gas line results in a fire.

D. a students cuts themselves with a scalpel.

13. **Which statement best defines negligence?**

A. failure to give oral instructions for those with reading disabilities

B. failure to exercise ordinary care

C. inability to supervise a large group of students.

D. reasonable anticipation that an event may occur

14. **Which item should always be used when using chemicals with noxious vapors?**

A. eye protection

B. face shield

C. fume hood

D. lab apron

15. **Identify the correct sequence of organization of living things.**

A. cell – organelle – organ – tissue – organ system – organism

B. cell – tissue – organ – organelle – organ system – organism

C. organelle – cell – tissue – organ – organ system – organism

D. organ system – tissue – organelle – cell – organism – organ

16. **Which of the following is not a required characteristic for something to be classified as living?**

A. movement

B. cellular structure

C. metabolism

D. reproduction

17. **Which kingdom is comprised of organisms made of one cell with no nuclear membrane?**

A. Monera

B. Protista

C. Fungi

D. Algae

18. Potassium chloride is an example of a(n)

A. non polar covalent bond

B. polar covalent bond

C. ionic bond

D. hydrogen bond

19. Which of the following is a monomer?

A. RNA

B. glycogen

C. DNA

D. amino acid

20. Which of the following are properties of water?

    I. High specific heat
    II. Strong ionic bonds
    III. Good solvent
    IV. High freezing point

A. I, III, IV

B. II and III

C. I and II

D. II, III, IV

21. Which does not affect enzyme rate?

A. increase of temperature

B. amount of substrate

C. pH

D. size of the cell

22. Sulfur oxides and nitrogen oxides in the environment react with water to cause

A. ammonia

B. acidic precipitation

C. sulfuric acid

D. global warming

23. The loss of an electron is _____ and the gain of an electron is _____.

A. oxidation, reduction

B. reduction, oxidation

C. glycolysis, photosynthesis

D. photosynthesis, glycolysis

24. The product of anaerobic respiration in animals is

A. carbon dioxide

B. lactic acid

C. pyruvate

D. ethyl alcohol

25. In the comparison of respiration to photosynthesis, which statement is true?

A. oxygen is a waste product in photosynthesis but not in respiration

B. glucose is produced in respiration but not in photosynthesis

C. carbon dioxide is formed in photosynthesis but not in respiration

D. water is formed in respiration but not in photosynthesis

26. Carbon dioxide is fixed in the form of glucose in

A. Krebs cycle

B. the light reactions

C. the dark reactions (Calvin cycle)

D. glycolysis

27. During the Kreb's cycle, 8 carrier molecules are formed. What are they?

A. 3 NADH, 3 FADH, 2 ATP

B. 6 NADH and 2 ATP

C. 4 $FADH_2$ and 4 ATP

D. 6 NADH and 2 $FADH_2$

28. Which of the following is not posttranscriptional processing?

A. 5' capping

B. intron splicing

C. polypeptide splicing

D. 3' polyadenylation

29. Polymerase chain reaction

A. is a group of polymerases

B. technique for amplifying DNA

C. primer for DNA synthesis

D. synthesis of polymerase

30. Homozygous individuals

A. have two different alleles

B. are of the same species

C. have the same features

D. have a pair of identical alleles

31. The two major ways to determine taxonomic classification are

  A. evolution and phylogeny

  B. reproductive success and evolution

  C. phylogeny and morphology

  D. size and color

32. Man's scientific name is Homo sapiens. Choose the proper classification beginning with kingdom and ending with order.

  A. Animalia, Vertebrata, Mammalia, Primate, Hominidae

  B. Animalia, Vertebrata, Chordata, Mammalia, Primate

  C. Animalia, Chordata, Vertebrata, Mammalia, Primate

  D. Chordata, Vertebrata, Primate, Homo, sapiens

33. The scientific name Canis familiaris refers to the animal's

  A. kingdom and phylum names

  B. genus and species names

  C. class and species names

  D. order and family names

34. Members of the same species

  A. look identical

  B. never change

  C. reproduce successfully among their group

  D. live in the same geographic location

35. What is necessary for diffusion to occur?

  A. carrier proteins

  B. energy

  C. a concentration gradient

  D. a membrane

36. Which is an example of the use of energy to move a substance through a membrane from areas of low concentration to areas of high concentration?

  A. osmosis

  B. active transport

  C. exocytosis

  D. phagocytosis

37. A plant cell is placed in salt water. The resulting movement of water out of the cell is called

    A. facilitated diffusion

    B. diffusion

    C. transpiration

    D. osmosis

38. As the amount of waste production increases in a cell, the rate of excretion

    A. slowly decreases

    B. remains the same

    C. increases

    D. stops due to cell death

39. A type of molecule not found in the membrane of an animal cell is

    A. phospholipid

    B. protein

    C. cellulose

    D. cholesterol

40. Which type of cell would contain the most mitochondria?

    A. muscle cell

    B. nerve cell

    C. epithelium

    D. blood cell

41. The first cells that evolved on earth were probably of which type?

    A. autotrophs

    B. eukaryotes

    C. heterotrophs

    D. prokaryotes

42. According to the fluid-mosaic model of the cell membrane, membranes are composed of

    A. phospholipid bilayers with proteins embedded in the layers

    B. one layer of phospholipids with cholesterol embedded in the layer

    C. two layers of protein with lipids embedded the layers

    D. DNA and fluid proteins

43. All the following statements regarding both a mitochondria and a chloroplast are correct except

A. they both produce energy over a gradient

B. they both have DNA and are capable of reproduction

C. they both transfer light energy to chemical energy

D. they both make ATP

44. This stage of mitosis includes cytokinesis or division of the cytoplasm and its organelles

A. anaphase

B. interphase

C. prophase

D. telophase

45. Replication of chromosomes occurs during which phase of the cell cycle?

A. prophase

B. interphase

C. metaphase

D. anaphase

46. Which statement regarding mitosis is correct?

A. diploid cells produce haploid cells for sexual reproduction

B. sperm and egg cells are produced

C. diploid cells produce diploid cells for growth and repair

D. it allows for greater genetic diversity

47. In a plant cell, telophase is described as

A. the time of chromosome doubling

B. cell plate formation

C. the time when crossing over occurs

D. cleavage furrow formation

48. Identify this stage of mitosis

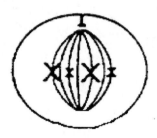

A. anaphase

B. metaphase

C. telophase

D. prophase

49. Identify this stage of mitosis

A. prophase

B. telophase

C. anaphase

D. metaphase

50. Identify this stage of mitosis

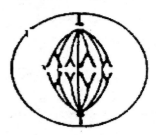

A. anaphase

B. metaphase

C. prophase

D. telophase

51. Oxygen is given off in the

A. light reactions of photosynthesis

B. dark reactions of photosynthesis

C. Kreb's cycle

D. reduction of NAD+ to NADH

52. In the electron transport chain, all the following are true except

A. it occurs in the mitochondrion

B. it does not make ATP directly

C. the net gain of energy is 30 ATP

D. most molecules in the electron transport chain are proteins.

53. The area of a DNA nucleotide that varies is the

A. deoxyribose

B. phosphate group

C. nitrogen base

D. sugar

54. A DNA strand has the base sequence of TCAGTA. Its DNA complement would have the following sequence

A. ATGACT

B. TCAGTA

C. AGUCAU

D. AGTCAT

55. Genes function in specifying the structure of which molecule?

A. carbohydrates

B. lipids

C. nucleic acids

D. proteins

56. What is the correct order of steps in protein synthesis?

A. transcription, then replication

B. transcription, then translation

C. translation, then transcription

D. replication, then translation

57. This carries amino acids to the ribosome in protein synthesis

A. messenger RNA

B. ribosomal RNA

C. transfer RNA

D. DNA

58. A protein is sixty amino acids in length. This requires a coded DNA sequence of how many nucleotides?

A. 20

B. 30

C. 120

D. 180

59. A DNA molecule has the sequence of ACTATG. What is the anticodon of this molecule?

A. UGAUAC

B. ACUAUG

C. TGATAC

D. ACTATG

60. The term "phenotype" refers to which of the following?

A. a condition which is heterozygous

B. the genetic makeup of an individual

C. a condition which is homozygous

D. how the genotype is expressed

61. The ratio of brown-eyed to blue-eyed children from the mating of a blue-eyed male to a heterozygous brown-eyed female would be expected to be which of the following?

A. 2:1

B. 1:1

C. 1:0

D. 1:2

62. The Law of Segregation defined by Mendel states that

A. when sex cells form, the two alleles that determine a trait will end up on different gametes

B. only one of two alleles is expressed in a heterozygous organism

C. the allele expressed is the dominant allele

D. alleles of one trait do not affect the inheritance of alleles on another chromosome

63. When a white flower is crossed with a red flower, incomplete dominance can be seen by the production of which of the following?

A. pink flowers

B. red flowers

C. white flowers

D. red and white flowers

64. Sutton observed that genes and chromosomes behaved the same. This led him to his theory which stated

A. that meiosis causes chromosome separation

B. that linked genes are able to separate

C. that genes and chromosomes have the same function

D. that genes are found on chromosomes

65. Amniocentesis is

A. a non-invasive technique for detecting genetic disorders

B. a bacterial infection

C. extraction of amniotic fluid

D. removal of fetal tissue

66. A child with type O blood has a father with type A blood and a mother with type B blood. The genotypes of the parents respectively would be which of the following?

A. AA and BO

B. AO and BO

C. AA and BB

D. AO and OO

67. Any change that affects the sequence of bases in a gene is called a (n)

A. deletion

B. polyploid

C. mutation

D. duplication

68. The *lac* operon

I. contains the *lac Z, lac Y, lac A* genes
II. converts glucose to lactose
III. contains a repressor
IV. is on when the repressor is activated

A. I

B. II

C. III and IV

D. I and III

69. Which of the following factors will affect the Hardy-Weinberg law of equilibrium, leading to evolutionary change?

A. no mutations

B. non-random mating

C. no immigration or emigration

D. Large population

70. If a population is in Hardy-Weinberg equilibrium and the frequency of the recessive allele is .3, what percentage of the population would be expected to be heterozygous?

A. 9%

B. 49%

C. 42%

D. 21%

71. Crossing over, which increases genetic diversity occurs during which stage(s)?

A. telophase II in meiosis

B. metaphase in mitosis

C. interphase in both mitosis and meiosis

D. prophase I in meiosis

72. Cancer cells divide extensively and invade other tissues. This continuous cell division is due to

A. density dependent inhibition

B. density independent inhibition

C. chromosome replication

D. Growth factors

73. Which process(es) results in a haploid chromosome number?

    A. both meiosis and mitosis

    B. mitosis

    C. meiosis

    D. replication and division

74. Segments of DNA can be transferred from the DNA of one organism to another through the use of which of the following?

    A. bacterial plasmids

    B. viruses

    C. chromosomes from frogs

    D. plant DNA

75. Which of the following is not true regarding restriction enzymes?

    A. they do not aid in recombination procedures

    B. they are used in genetic engineering

    C. they are named after the bacteria in which they naturally occur

    D. they identify and splice certain base sequences on DNA

76. A virus that can remain dormant until a certain environmental condition causes its rapid increase is said to be

    A. lytic

    B. benign

    C. saprophytic

    D. lysogenic

77. Which is not considered to be a morphological type of bacteria?

    A. obligate

    B. coccus

    C. spirillum

    D. bacillus

78. Antibiotics are effective in fighting bacterial infections due to their ability to

    A. interfere with DNA replication in the bacteria

    B. prevent the formation of new cell walls in the bacteria

    C. disrupt the ribosome of the bacteria

    D. All of the above.

79. Bacteria commonly reproduce by a process called binary fission. Which of the following best defines this process?

A. viral vectors carry DNA to new bacteria

B. DNA from one bacterium enters another

C. DNA doubles and the bacterial cell divides

D. DNA from dead cells is absorbed into bacteria

80. All of the following are examples of a member of Kingdom Fungi except

A. mold

B. algae

C. mildew

D. mushrooms

81. Protists are classified into major groups according to

A. their method of obtaining nutrition

B. reproduction

C. metabolism

D. their form and function

82. In comparison to protist cells, moneran cells

I. are usually smaller
II. evolved later
III. are more complex
IV. contain more organelles

A. I

B. I and II

C. II and III

D. I and IV

83. Spores characterize the reproduction mode for which of the following group of plants?

A. algae

B. flowering plants

C. conifers

D. ferns

84. Water movement to the top of a twenty foot tree is most likely due to which principle?

A. osmostic pressure

B. xylem pressure

C. capillarity

D. transpiration

85. What are the stages of development from the egg to the plant?

   A. morphogenesis, growth, and cellular differentiation

   B. cell differentiation, growth, and morphogenesis

   C. growth, morphogenesis, and cellular differentiation

   D. growth, cellular differentiation, and morphogensis

86. In angiosperms, the food for the developing plant is found in which of the following structures?

   A. ovule

   B. endosperm

   C. male gametophyte

   D. cotyledon

87. The process in which pollen grains are released from the anthers is called

   A. pollination

   B. fertilization

   C. blooming

   D. dispersal

88. Which of the following is not a characteristic of a monocot?

   A. parallel veins in leaves

   B. petals of flowers occur in multiples of 4 or 5

   C. one seed leaf

   D. vascular tissue scattered throughout the stem

89. What controls gas exchange on the bottom of a plant leaf?

   A. stomata

   B. epidermis

   C. collenchyma and schlerenchyma

   D. palisade mesophyll

90. How are angiosperms different from other groups of plants?

   A. presence of flowers and fruits

   B. production of spores for reproduction

   C. true roots and stems

   D. seed production

91. Generations of plants alternate between

A. angiosperms and bryophytes

B. flowering and nonflowering stages

C. seed bearing and spore bearing plants

D. haploid and diploid stages

92. Double fertilization refers to which choice of the following?

A. two sperm fertilizing one egg

B. fertilization of a plant by gametes from two separate plants

C. two sperm enter the plant embryo sac; one sperm fertilizes the egg, the other forms the endosperm

D. the production of non-identical twins through fertilization of two separate eggs

93. Characteristics of coelomates include:

I. no true digestive system
II. two germ layers
III. true fluid filled cavity
IV. three germ layers

A. I

B. II and IV

C. IV

D. III and IV

94. Which phylum accounts for 85% of all animal species?

A. Nematoda

B. Chordata

C. Arthropoda

D. Cnidaria

95. Which is the correct statement regarding the human nervous system and the human endocrine system?

A. the nervous system maintains homeostasis whereas the endocrine system does not

B. endocrine glands produce neurotransmitters whereas nerves produce hormones

C. nerve signals travel on neurons whereas hormones travel through the blood

D. he nervous system involves chemical transmission whereas the endocrine system does not

96. A muscular adaptation to move food through the digestive system is called

A. peristalsis

B. passive transport

C. voluntary action

D. bulk transport

97. The role of neurotransmitters in nerve action is

A. turn off sodium pump

B. turn off calcium pump

C. send impulse to neuron

D. send impulse to the body

98. Fats are broken down by which substance?

A. bile produced in the gall bladder

B. lipase produced in the gall bladder

C. glucagons produced in the liver

D. bile produced in the liver

99. Fertilization in humans usually occurs in the

A. uterus

B. ovary

C. fallopian tubes

D. vagina

100. All of the following are found in the dermis layer of skin except

A. sweat glands

B. keratin

C. hair follicles

D. blood vessels

101. Which is the correct sequence of embryonic development in a frog?

A. cleavage – blastula – gastrula

B. cleavage – gastrula – blastula

C. blastula – cleavage – gastrula

D. gastrula – blastula – cleavage

102. Food is carried through the digestive tract by a series of wave-like contractions. This process is called

A. peristalsis

B. chyme

C. digestion

D. absorption

103. Movement is possible by the action of muscles pulling on

A. skin

B. bones

C. joints

D. ligaments

104. All of the following are functions of the skin except

A. storage

B. protection

C. sensation

D. regulation of temperature

105. Hormones are essential to the regulation of reproduction. What organ is responsible for the release of hormones for sexual maturity?

A. pituitary gland

B. hypothalamus

C. pancreas

D. thyroid gland

106. A bicyclist has a heart rate of 110 beats per minute and a stroke volume of 85 mL per beat. What is the cardiac output?

A. 9.35 L/min

B. 1.29 L/min

C. 0.772 L/min

D. 129 L/min

107. After sea turtles are hatched on the beach, they start the journey to the ocean. This is due to

A. innate behavior

B. territoriality

C. the tide

D. learned behavior

108. A school age boy had the chicken pox as a baby. He will most likely not get this disease again because of

A. passive immunity

B. vaccination

C. antibiotics

D. active immunity

109. High humidity and temperature stability are present in which of the following biomes?

A. taiga

B. deciduous forest

C. desert

D. tropical rain forest

110. The biological species concept applies to

A. asexual organisms

B. extinct organisms

C. sexual organisms

D. fossil organisms

111. Which term is not associated with the water cycle?

A. precipitation

B. transpiration

C. fixation

D. evaporation

112. **All of the following are density independent factors that affect a population except**

    A. temperature

    B. rainfall

    C. predation

    D. soil nutrients

113. **In the growth of a population, the increase is exponential until carrying capacity is reached. This is represented by a (n)**

    A. S curve

    B. J curve

    C. M curve

    D. L curve

114. **Primary succession occurs after**

    A. nutrient enrichment

    B. a forest fire

    C. bare rock is exposed after a water table recedes

    D. a housing development is built

115. **Crabgrass – grasshopper – frog – snake – eagle If DDT were present in an ecosystem, which organism would have the highest concentration in its system?**

    A. grasshopper

    B. eagle

    C. frog

    D. crabgrass

116. **Which trophic level has the highest ecological efficiency?**

    A. decomposers

    B. producers

    C. tertiary consumers

    D. secondary consumers

117. **A clownfish is protected by the sea anemone's tentacles. In turn, the anemone receives uneaten food from the clownfish. This is an example of**

    A. mutualism

    B. parasitism

    C. commensalisms

    D. competition

118. If the niches of two species overlap, what usually results?

A. a symbiotic relationship

B. cooperation

C. competition

D. a new species

119. Oxygen created in photosynthesis comes from the breakdown of

A. carbon dioxide

B. water

C. glucose

D. carbon monoxide

120. Which photosystem makes ATP?

A. photosystem I

B. photosystem II

C. photosystem III

D. photosystem IV

121. All of the following gasses made up the primitive atmosphere except

A. ammonia

B. methane

C. oxygen

D. hydrogen

122. The Endosymbiotic theory states that

A. eukaryotes arose from prokaryotes

B. animals evolved in close relationships with one another

C. the prokaryotes arose from eukaryotes

D. life arose from inorganic compounds

123. Which aspect of science does not support evolution?

A. comparative anatomy

B. organic chemistry

C. comparison of DNA among organisms

D. analogous structures

124. Evolution occurs in

A. individuals

B. populations

C. organ systems

D. cells

125. Which process contributes to the large variety of living things in the world today?

   A. meiosis

   B. asexual reproduction

   C. mitosis

   D. alternation of generations

126. The wing of bird, human arm and whale flipper have the same bone structure. These are called

   A. polymorphic structures

   B. homologous structures

   C. vestigial structures

   D. analogous structures

127. Which biome is the most prevalent on Earth?

   A. marine

   B. desert

   C. savanna

   D. tundra

128. Which of the following is not an abiotic factor?

   A. temperature

   B. rainfall

   C. soil quality

   D. bacteria

129. DNA synthesis results in a strand that is synthesized continuously. This is the

   A. lagging strand

   B. leading strand

   C. template strand

   D. complementary strand

130. Using a gram staining technique, it is observed that E. coli stains pink. It is therefore

   A. gram positive

   B. dead

   C. gram negative

   D. gram neutral

131. A light microscope has an ocular of 10X and an objective of 40X. What is the total magnification?

   A. 400X

   B. 30X

   C. 50X

   D. 4000X

132. Three plants were grown. The following data was taken. Determine the mean growth.
Plant 1: 10cm Plant 2: 20cm
Plant 3: 15cm

A. 5 cm

B. 45 cm

C. 12 cm

D. 15 cm

133. Electrophoresis separates DNA on the basis of

A. amount of current

B. molecular size

C. positive charge of the molecule

D. solubility of the gel

134. The reading of a meniscus in a graduated cylinder is done at the

A. top of the meniscus

B. middle of the meniscus

C. bottom of the meniscus

D. closest whole number

135. Two hundred plants were grown. Fifty plants died. What percentage of the plants survived?

A. 40%

B. 25%

C. 75%

D. 50%

136. Which is not a correct statement regarding the use of a light microscope?

A. carry the microscope with two hands

B. store on the low power objective

C. clean all lenses with lens paper

D. Focus first on high power

137. Spectrophotometry utilizes the principle of

A. light transmission

B. molecular weight

C. solubility of the substance

D. electrical charges

138. Chromotography is most often associated with the separation of

A. nutritional elements

B. DNA

C. proteins

D. plant pigments

139. A genetic engineering advancement in the medical field is

A. gene therapy

B. pesticides

C. degradation of harmful chemicals

D. antibiotics

140. Which scientists are credited with the discovery of the structure of DNA?

A. Hershey & Chase

B. Sutton & Morgan

C. Watson & Crick

D. Miller & Fox

141. Negatively charged particles that circle the nucleus of an atom are called

A. neutrons

B. neutrinos

C. electrons

D. protons

142. The shape of a cell depends on its

A. function

B. structure

C. age

D. size

143. The most ATP is generated through

A. fermentation

B. glycolysis

C. chemiosmosis

D. Krebs cycle

144. In DNA, adenine bonds with _____, while cytosine bonds with _____.

A. thymine/guanine

B. adenine/cytosine

C. cytosine/adenine

D. guanine/thymine

145. The individual parts of cells are best studied using a (n)

A. ultracentrifuge

B. phase-contrast microscope

C. CAT scan

D. electron microscope

146. Thermoacidophiles are

    A. prokaryotes

    B. eukaryotes

    C. bacteria

    D. archaea

147. Which of the following is not a type of fiber that makes up the cytoskeleton?

    A. vacuoles

    B. microfilaments

    C. microtubules

    D. intermediate filaments

148. Viruses are made of

    A. a protein coat surrounding a nucleic acid

    B. DNA, RNA and a cell wall

    C. a nucleic acid surrounding a protein coat

    D. protein surrounded by DNA

149. Reproductive isolation results in

    A. extinction

    B. migration

    C. follilization

    D. speciation

150. This protein structure consists of the coils and folds of polypeptide chains. Which is it?

    A. secondary structure

    B. quaternary structure

    C. tertiary structure

    D. primary structure

Answer Key

1. C	32. C	63. A	94. C	125. A
2. C	33. B	64. D	95. C	126. B
3. B	34. C	65. C	96. A	127. A
4. D	35. C	66. B	97. A	128. D
5. C	36. B	67. C	98. D	129. B
6. D	37. D	68. D	99. C	130. C
7. D	38. C	69. B	100. B	131. A
8. C	39. C	70. C	101. A	132. D
9. D	40. A	71. D	102. A	133. B
10. D	41. D	72. B	103. B	134. C
11. A	42. A	73. C	104. A	135. C
12. A	43. C	74. A	105. B	136. D
13. B	44. D	75. A	106. A	137. A
14. C	45. B	76. D	107. A	138. D
15. C	46. C	77. A	108. D	139. A
16. A	47. B	78. D	109. D	140. C
17. A	48. B	79. C	110. C	141. C
18. C	49. B	80. B	111. C	142. A
19. D	50. A	81. D	112. C	143. C
20. A	51. A	82. A	113. A	144. A
21. D	52. C	83. D	114. C	145. D
22. B	53. C	84. D	115. B	146. D
23. A	54. D	85. C	116. B	147. A
24. B	55. D	86. B	117. A	148. A
25. A	56. B	87. A	118. C	149. D
26. C	57. C	88. B	119. B	150. A
27. D	58. D	89. A	120. A	
28. C	59. B	90. A	121. C	
29. B	60. D	91. D	122. A	
30. D	61. B	92. C	123. B	
31. C	62. A	93. D	124. B	

Rationales for Sample Questions

1. **A student designed a science project testing the effects of light and water on plant growth. You would recommend that she**

   A. manipulate the temperature
      as well.
   B. also alter the pH of the water as another variable.
   C. omit either water or light as a variable.
   D. also alter the light concentration as another variable.

C. In science, experiments should be designed so that only one variable is manipulated at a time.

2. **Identify the control in the following experiment. A student had four plants grown under the following conditions and was measuring photosynthetic rate by measuring mass. 2 plants in 50% light and 2 plants in 100% light.**

   A. plants grown with no added nutrients
   B. plants grown in the dark
   C plants in 100% light
   D. plants in 50% light

C. The 100% light plants are those that the student will be comparing the 50% plants to. This will be the control.

3. **In an experiment measuring the growth of bacteria at different temperatures, identify the independent variable.**

   A. growth of number of colonies
   B. temperature
   C. type of bacteria used
   D. light intensity

B. The independent variable is controlled by the experimenter. Here, the temperature is controlled to determine its effect on the growth of bacteria (dependent variable).

4. A scientific theory

  A. proves scientific accuracy.
  B. is never rejected.
  C. results in a medical breakthrough.
  D. may be altered at a later time.

D. Scientific theory is usually accepted and verified information but can always be changed at anytime.

5. Which is the correct order of methodology? 1) testing revised explanation, 2) setting up a controlled experiment to test explanation, 3) drawing a conclusion, 4) suggesting an explanation for observations, and 5) compare observed results to hypothesized results

  A. 4, 2, 3, 1, 5
  B. 3, 1, 4, 2, 5
  C. 4, 2, 5, 1, 3
  D. 2, 5, 4, 1, 3

C. The first step in scientific inquiry is posing a question to be answered. Next, a hypothesis is formed to provide a plausible explanation. An experiment is then proposed and performed to test this hypothesis. A comparison between the predicted and observed results is the next step. Conclusions are then formed and it is determined whether the hypothesis is correct or incorrect. If incorrect, the next step is to form a new hypothesis and the process is repeated.

6. Given a choice, which is the most desirable method of heating a substance in the lab?

  A. alcohol burner
  B. gas burner
  C. bunsen burner
  D. hot plate

D. A hotplate is the only heat source from the choices above that does not have an open flame. The use of a hot plate will reduce the risk of fire and injury to students.

7. **Biological waste should be disposed of**

   A. in the trash can.
   B. under a fume hood.
   C. in the broken glass box.
   D. in an autoclavable biohazard bag.

D. Biological material should never be stored near food or water used for human consumption. All biological material should be appropriately labeled. All blood and body fluids should be put in a well-contained container with a secure lid to prevent leaking. All biological waste should be disposed of in biological hazardous waste bags.

8. **Chemicals should be stored**

   A. in a cool dark room.
   B. in a dark room.
   C. according to their reactivity with other substances.
   D. in a double locked room.

C. All chemicals should be stored with other chemicals of similar reactivity. Failure to do so could result in an undesirable chemical reaction.

9. **Given the choice of lab activities, which would you omit?**

   A. a genetics experiment tracking the fur color of mice
   B. dissecting a preserved fetal pig
   C. a lab relating temperature to respiration rate using live goldfish.
   D. pithing a frog to see the action of circulation

D. The use of live vertebrate organisms in a way that may harm the animal is prohibited. The observation of fur color in mice is not harmful to the animal and the use of live goldfish is acceptable because they are invertebrates. The dissection of a fetal pig is acceptable if it comes from a known origin.

10. Who should be notified in the case of a serious chemical spill?

    I. the custodian
    II. The fire department
    III. the chemistry teacher
    IV. the administration

    A. I
    B. II
    C. II and III
    D. II and IV

D. For large spills, the school administration and the local fire department should be notified.

11. The "Right to Know" law states

    A. the inventory of toxic chemicals checked against the "Substance List" be available.
    B. that students are to be informed on alternatives to dissection.
    C. that science teachers are to be informed of student allergies.
    D. that students are to be informed of infectious microorganisms used in lab.

A. The right to know law pertains to chemical substances in the lab. Employees should check the material safety data sheets and the substance list for potential hazards in the lab.

12. In which situation would a science teacher be liable?

    A. a teacher leaves to receive an emergency phone call and a student slips and falls.
    B. a student removes their goggles and gets dissection fluid in their eye.
    C. a faulty gas line results in a fire.
    D. a students cuts themselves with a scalpel.

A. A teacher has an obligation to be present in the lab at all times. If the teacher needs to leave, an appropriate substitute is needed.

13. Which statement best defines negligence?

A. failure to give oral instructions for those with reading disabilities
B. failure to exercise ordinary care
C. inability to supervise a large group of students.
D. reasonable anticipation that an event may occur

B. Negligence is the failure to exercise ordinary or reasonable care.

14. Which item should always be used when using chemicals with noxious vapors?

A. eye protection
B. face shield
C. fume hood
D. lab apron

C. Fume hoods are designed to protect the experimenter from chemical fumes. The three other choices do not prevent chemical fumes from entering the respiratory system.

15. Identify the correct sequence of organization of living things.

A. cell – organelle – organ system – tissue – organ – organism
B. cell – tissue – organ – organ system – organelle – organism
C. organelle – cell – tissue – organ – organ system – organism
D. tissue – organelle – organ – cell – organism – organ system

C. An organism, such as a human, is comprised of several organ systems such as the circulatory and nervous systems. These organ systems consist of many organs including the heart and the brain. These organs are made of tissue such as cardiac muscle. Tissues are made up of cells, which contain organelles like the mitochondria and the Golgi apparatus.

16. Which is not a characteristic of living things?

A. movement
B. cellular structure
C. metabolism
D. reproduction

A. Movement is not a characteristic of life. Viruses are considered non-living organisms but have the ability to move from cell to cell in its host organism.

17. Which kingdom is comprised of organisms made of one cell with no nuclear membrane?

    A. Monera
    B. Protista
    C. Fungi
    D. Algae

A. Monera is the only kingdom that is made up of unicellular organisms with no nucleus. Algae is a protest because it is made up of one type of tissue and it has a nucleus.

18. Potassium chloride is an example of a(n)

    A. non polar covalent bond
    B. polar covalent bond
    C. ionic bond
    D. hydrogen bond

C. Ionic bonds are formed when one electron is stripped away from its atom to join another atom. Ionic compounds are called salts and potassium chloride is a salt; therefore, potassium chloride is an example of an ionic bond.

19. Which of the following is a monomer?

    A. RNA
    B. glycogen
    C. DNA
    D. amino acid

D. A monomer is the simplest unit of structure for a particular macromolecule. Amino acids are the basic unit that comprises a protein. RNA and DNA are polymers consisting of nucleotides and glycogen is a polymer consisting of many molecules of glucose.

20. Which of the following are properties of water?

    I. High specific heat
    II. Strong ionic bonds
    III.Good solvent
    IV.High freezing point

    A. I, III, IV
    B. II and III
    C. I and II
    D. II, III, IV

A. All are properties of water except strong ionic bonds. Water is held together by polar covalent bonds between hydrogen and oxygen.

21. Which does not affect enzyme rate?

    A. increase of temperature
    B. amount of substrate
    C. pH
    D. size of the cell

D. Temperature and pH can affect the rate of reaction of an enzyme. The amount of substrate affects the enzyme as well. The enzyme acts on the substrate. The more substrate, the slower the enzyme rate. Therefore, the only chance left is D, the size of the cell, which has no effect on enzyme rate.

22. Sulfur oxides and nitrogen oxides in the environment react with water to cause

    A. ammonia
    B. acidic precipitation
    C. sulfuric acid
    D. global warming

B. Acidic precipitation is rain, snow, or fog with a pH less than 5.6. It is caused by sulfur oxides and nitrogen oxides that react with water in the air to form acids that fall down to Earth as precipitation.

23. The loss of an electron is _____ and the gain of an electron is _____.

    A. oxidation, reduction
    B. reduction, oxidation
    C. glycolysis, photosynthesis
    D. photosynthesis, glycolysis

A. Oxidation-reduction reactions are also known as redox reactions. In respiration, energy is released by the transfer of electrons by this process. The oxidation phase of this reaction is the loss of an electron and the reduction phase is the gain of an electron.

24. The product of anaerobic respiration in animals is

    A. carbon dioxide
    B. lactic acid
    C. pyruvate
    D. ethyl alcohol

B. In anaerobic lactic acid fermentation, pyruvate is reduced by NADH to form lactic acid. This is the anaerobic process in animals. Alcoholic fermentation is the anaerobic process in yeast and some bacteria resulting in ethyl alcohol. Carbon dioxide and pyruvate are the products of aerobic respiration.

25. In the comparison of respiration to photosynthesis, which statement is true?

    A. oxygen is a waste product in photosynthesis but not in respiration
    B. glucose is produced in respiration but not in photosynthesis
    C. carbon dioxide is formed in photosynthesis but not in respiration
    D. water is formed in respiration but not in photosynthesis

A. In photosynthesis, water is split and the oxygen is given off as a waste product. In respiration, water and carbon dioxide are the waste products.

26. Carbon dioxide is fixed in the form of glucose in

    A. Krebs cycle
    B. the light reactions
    C. the dark reactions (Calvin cycle)
    D. glycolysis

C. The ATP produced during the light reaction is needed to convert carbon dioxide to glucose in the Calvin cycle.

27. During the Kreb's cycle, 8 carrier molecules are formed. What are they?

    A. 3 NADH, 3 FADH, 2 ATP
    B. 6 NADH and 2 ATP
    C. 4 $FADH_2$ and 4 ATP
    D. 6 NADH and 2 $FADH_2$

D. For each molecule of CoA that enters the Kreb's cycle, you get 3 NADH and 1 $FADH_2$. There are 2 molecules of CoA so the total yield is 6 NADH and 2 $FADH_2$ during the Kreb's cycle.

28. Which of the following is not posttranscriptional processing?

    A. 5' capping
    B. intron splicing
    C. polypeptide splicing
    D. 3' polyadenylation

C. The removal of segments of polypeptides is a posttranslational process. The other three are methods of posttranscriptional processing.

29. Polymerase chain reaction

    A. is a group of polymerases
    B. technique for amplifying DNA
    C. primer for DNA synthesis
    D. synthesis of polymerase

B. PCR is a technique in which a piece of DNA can be amplified into billions of copies within a few hour.

30. **Homozygous individuals**

    A. have two different alleles
    B. are of the same species
    C. have the same features
    D. have a pair of identical alleles

D. Homozygous individuals have a pair of identical alleles and heterozygous individuals have two different alleles.

31. **The two major ways to determine taxonomic classification are**

    A. evolution and phylogeny
    B. reproductive success and evolution
    C. phylogeny and morphology
    D. size and color

C. Taxonomy is based on structure (morphology) and evolutionary relationships (phylogeny).

32. **Man's scientific name is Homo sapiens. Choose the proper classification beginning with kingdom and ending with order.**

    A. Animalia, Vertebrata, Mammalia, Primate, Hominidae
    B. Animalia, Vertebrata, Chordata, Mammalia, Primate
    C. Animalia, Chordata, Vertebrata, Mammalia, Primate
    D. Chordata, Vertebrata, Primate, Homo, sapiens

C. The order of classification for humans is as follows: Kingdom, Animalia; Phylum, Chordata; Subphylum, Vertebrata; Class, Mammalia; Order, Primate; Family, Hominadae; Genus, Homo; Species, sapiens.

33. **The scientific name Canis familiaris refers to the animal's**

    A. kingdom and phylum names
    B. genus and species names
    C. class and species names
    D. order and family names

B. Each species is scientifically known by a two-part name, or binomial. The first word in the name is the genus and the second word is its specific epithet (species name).

34.Members of the same species

A. look identical
B. never change
C. reproduce successfully among their group
D. live in the same geographic location

C. Species are defined by the ability to successfully reproduce with members of their own kind.

35. What is necessary for diffusion to occur?

A. carrier proteins
B. energy
C. a concentration gradient
D. a membrane

C. Diffusion is the ability of molecules to move from areas of high concentration to areas of low concentration (a concentration gradient).

36. Which is an example of the use of energy to move a substance through a membrane from areas of low concentration to areas of high concentration?

A. osmosis
B. active transport
C. exocytosis
D. phagocytosis

B. Active transport can move substances with or against the concentration gradient. This energy requiring process allows for molecules to move from areas of low concentration to high concentration areas.

37.A plant cell is placed in salt water. The resulting movement of water out of the cell is called

A. facilitated diffusion
B. diffusion
C. transpiration
D. osmosis

D. Osmosis is simply the diffusion of water across a semi-permeable membrane. Water will diffuse out of the cell if there is less water on the outside of the cell.

38. As the amount of waste production increases in a cell, the rate of excretion

    A. slowly decreases
    B. remains the same
    C. increases
    D. stops due to cell death

C. Homeostasis is the control of the differences between internal and external environments. Excretion is the homeostatic system that regulates the amount of waste in a cell. As the amount of waste increases, the rate of excretion will increase to maintain homeostasis.

39. A type of molecule not found in the membrane of an animal cell is

    A. phospholipid
    B. protein
    C. cellulose
    D. cholesterol

C. Phospholipids, protein, and cholesterol are all found in animal cells. Cellulose, however, is only found in plant cells.

40. Which type of cell would contain the most mitochondria?

    A. muscle cell
    B. nerve cell
    C. epithelium
    D. blood cell

A. Mitochondria are the site of cellular respiration where ATP is made. Muscle cells have the most mitochondria because they use a great deal of energy.

41. The first cells that evolved on earth were probably of which type?

    A. autotrophs
    B. eukaryotes
    C. heterotrophs
    D. prokaryotes

D. Prokaryotes date back to 3.5 billion years ago in the first fossil record. Their ability to adapt to the environment allows them to thrive in a wide variety of habitats.

42. According to the fluid-mosaic model of the cell membrane, membranes are composed of

    A. phospholipid bilayers with proteins embedded in the layers
    B. one layer of phospholipids with cholesterol embedded in the layer
    C. two layers of protein with lipids embedded the layers
    D. DNA and fluid proteins

A. Cell membranes are composed of two phospholipids with their hydrophobic tails sandwiched between their hydrophilic heads, creating a lipid bilayer. The membrane contains proteins embedded in the layer (integral proteins) and proteins on the surface (peripheral proteins).

43. All the following statements regarding both a mitochondria and a chloroplast are correct except

    A. they both produce energy over a gradient
    B. they both have DNA and are capable of reproduction
    C. they both transfer light energy to chemical energy
    D. they both make ATP

C. Cellular respiration does not transfer light energy to chemical energy. Cellular respiration transfers electrons to release energy. Photosynthesis utilizes light energy to produce chemical energy.

44. This stage of mitosis includes cytokinesis or division of the cytoplasm and its organelles

    A. anaphase
    B. interphase
    C. prophase
    D. telophase

D. The last stage of the mitotic phase is telophase. Here, the two nuclei form with a full set of DNA each. The cell is pinched into two cells and cytokinesis, or division of the cytoplasm and organelles, occurs.

45. Replication of chromosomes occurs during which phase of the cell cycle?

   A. prophase
   B. interphase
   C. metaphase
   D. anaphase

B. Interphase is the stage where the cell grows and copies the chromosomes in preparation for the mitotic phase.

46. Which statement regarding mitosis is correct?

   A. diploid cells produce haploid cells for sexual reproduction
   B. sperm and egg cells are produced
   C. diploid cells produce diploid cells for growth and repair
   D. it allows for greater genetic diversity

C. The purpose of mitotic cell division is to provide growth and repair in body (somatic) cells. The cells begin as diploid and produce diploid cells.

47. In a plant cell, telophase is described as

   A. the time of chromosome doubling
   B. cell plate formation
   C. the time when crossing over occurs
   D. cleavage furrow formation

B. During plant cell telophase, a cell plate is observed whereas a cleavage furrow is formed in animal cells.

48. **Identify this stage of mitosis**

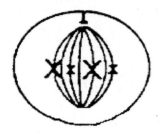

A. anaphase
B. metaphase
C. telophase
D. prophase

B. During metaphase, the centromeres are at opposite ends of the cell. Here the chromosomes are aligned with one another.

49. **Identify this stage of mitosis**

A. prophase
B. telophase
C. anaphase
D. metaphase

B. Telophase is the last stage of mitosis. Here, two nuclei become visible and the nuclear membrane resembles.

50. Identify this stage of mitosis

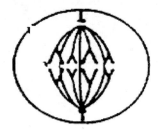

    A. anaphase
    B. metaphase
    C. prophase
    D. telophase

A. During anaphase, the centromeres split in half and homologous chromosomes separate.

51. Oxygen is given off in the

    A. light reactions of photosynthesis
    B. dark reactions of photosynthesis
    C. Krebs cycle
    D. reduction of NAD+ to NADH

A. The conversion of solar energy to chemical energy occurs in the light reactions. Electrons are transferred by the absorption of light by chlorophyll and causes water to split, releasing oxygen as a waste product.

52. In the electron transport chain, all the following are true except

    A. it occurs in the mitochondrion
    B. it does not make ATP directly
    C. the net gain of energy is 30 ATP
    D. most molecules in the electron
         transport chain are proteins.

C. The end result of the electron transport chain is 34 molecules of ATP.

53.The area of a DNA nucleotide that varies is the

    A. deoxyribose
    B. phosphate group
    C. nitrogen base
    D. sugar

C. DNA is made of a 5 carbon sugar (deoxyribose), a phosphate group, and a nitrogenous base. There are four nitrogenous bases in DNA that allow for the four different nucleotides.

54.A DNA strand has the base sequence of TCAGTA. Its DNA complement would have the following sequence

    A. ATGACT
    B. TCAGTA
    C. AGUCAU
    D. AGTCAT

D. The complement strand to a single strand DNA molecule has a complementary sequence to the template strand. T pairs with A and C pairs with G. Therefore, the complement to TCAGTA is AGTCAT.

55.Genes function in specifying the structure of which molecule?

    A. carbohydrates
    B. lipids
    C. nucleic acids
    D. proteins

D. Genes contain the sequence of nucleotides that code for amino acids. Amino acids are the building blocks of protein.

56.What is the correct order of steps in protein synthesis?

    A. transcription, then replication
    B. transcription, then translation
    C. translation, then transcription
    D. replication, then translation

B. A DNA strand first undergoes transcription to get a complementary mRNA strand. Translation of the mRNA strand then occurs to result in the tRNA adding the appropriate amino acid for an ending product of a protein.

57. This carries amino acids to the ribosome in protein synthesis

    A. messenger RNA
    B. ribosomal RNA
    C. transfer RNA
    D. DNA

C. The tRNA molecule is specific for a particular amino acid. The tRNA has an anticodon sequence that is complementary to the codon. This specifies where the tRNA places the amino acid in protein synthesis.

58. A protein is sixty amino acids in length. This requires a coded DNA sequence of how many nucleotides?

    A. 20
    B. 30
    C. 120
    D. 180

D. Each amino acid codon consists of 3 nucleotides. If there are 60 amino acids in a protein, then 60 x 30 = 180 nucleotides.

59. A DNA molecule has the sequence of ACTATG. What is the anticodon of this molecule?

    A. UGAUAC
    B. ACUAUG
    C. TGATAC
    D. ACTATG

B. The DNA is first transcribed into mRNA. Here, the DNA has the sequence ACTATG; therefore the complementary mRNA sequence is UGAUAC (remember, in RNA, T are U). This mRNA sequence is the codon. The anticodon is the complement to the codon. The anticodon sequence will be ACUAUG (remember, the anticodon is tRNA, so U is present instead of T).

60. The term "phenotype" refers to which of the following?

A. a condition which is heterozygous
B. the genetic makeup of an individual
C. a condition which is homozygous
D. how the genotype is expressed

D. Phenotype is the physical appearance of an organism due to its genetic makeup (genotype).

61. The ratio of brown-eyed to blue-eyed children from the mating of a blue-eyed male to a heterozygous brown-eyed female would be expected to be which of the following?

A. 2:1
B. 1:1
C. 1:0
D. 1:2

B. Use a Punnet square to determine the ratio.

	b	b
B	Bb	Bb
b	bb	bb

B = brown eyes, b = blue eyes

Female genotype is on the side and the male genotype is across the top.

The female is heterozygous and her phenotype is brown eyes. This means the dominant allele is for brown eyes. The male expresses the homozygous recessive allele for blue eyes. Their children are expected to have a ratio of brown eyes to blue eyes of 2:2; or 1:1.

62. The Law of Segregation defined by Mendel states that

A. when sex cells form, the two alleles that determine a trait will end up on different gametes
B. only one of two alleles is expressed in a heterozygous organism
C. the allele expressed is the dominant allele
D. alleles of one trait do not affect the inheritance of alleles on another chromosome

A. The law of segregation states that the two alleles for each trait segregate into different gametes.

63. When a white flower is crossed with a red flower, incomplete dominance can be seen by the production of which of the following?

    A. pink flowers
    B. red flowers
    C. white flowers
    D. red and white flowers

A. Incomplete dominance is when the F_1 generation results in an appearance somewhere between the parents. Red flowers crossed with white flowers results in an F_1 generation with pink flowers.

64. Sutton observed that genes and chromosomes behaved the same. This led him to his theory which stated

    A. that meiosis causes chromosome separation
    B. that linked genes are able to separate
    C. that genes and chromosomes have the same function
    D. that genes are found on chromosomes

D. Sutton observed how mitosis and meiosis confirmed Mendel's theory on "factors." His Chromosome Theory states that genes are located on chromosomes.

65. Amniocentesis is

    A. a non-invasive technique for detecting genetic disorders
    B. a bacterial infection
    C. extraction of amniotic fluid
    D. removal of fetal tissue

C. Amniocentesis is a procedure in which a needle is inserted into the uterus to extract some of the amniotic fluid surrounding the fetus. Some genetic disorders can be detected by chemicals in the fluid.

66. A child with type O blood has a father with type A blood and a mother with type B blood. The genotypes of the parents respectively would be which of the following?

A. AA and BO
B. AO and BO
C. AA and BB
D. AO and OO

B. Type O blood has 2 recessive O genes. A child receives one allele from each parent; therefore each parent in this example must have an O allele. The father has type A blood with a genotype of AO and the mother has type B blood with a genotype of BO.

67. Any change that affects the sequence of bases in a gene is called a(n)

A. deletion
B. polyploid
C. mutation
D. duplication

C. A mutation is an inheritable change in DNA. They may be errors in replication or a spontaneous rearrangement of one ore more segments of DNA. Deletion and duplication are type of mutations. Polyploidy is when and organism has more than two complete chromosome sets.

68. The *lac* operon

I. contains the *lac Z, lac Y, lac A* genes
II. converts glucose to lactose
III. contains a repressor
IV. is on when the repressor is activated

A. I
B. II
C. III and IV
D. I and III

D. The *lac* operon contains the genes that encode for the enzymes used to convert lactose into fuel. It contains three genes: *lac A, lac Z,* and *lac Y*. It also contains a promoter and repressor. When the repressor is activated, the operon is off.

69. Which of the following factors will affect the Hardy-Weinberg law of equilibrium, leading to evolutionary change?

    A. no mutations
    B. non-random mating
    C. no immigration or emigration
    D. Large population

B. There are five requirements to keep the Hardy-Weinberg equilibrium stable: no mutation, no selection pressures, an isolated population, a large population, and random mating.

70. If a population is in Hardy-Weinberg equilibrium and the frequency of the recessive allele is 0.3, what percentage of the population would be expected to be heterozygous?

    A. 9%
    B. 49%
    C. 42%
    D. 21%

C. 0.3 is the value of q. Therefore, $q^2 = 0.09$. According to the Hardy-Weinberg equation, $1 = p + q$.

$1 = p + 0.3$.
$p = 0.7$
$p^2 = 0.49$

Next, plug q^2 and p^2 into the equation $1 = p^2 + 2pq + q^2$.

$1 = 0.49 + 2pq + 0.09$ (where 2pq is the number of heterozygotes).
$1 = 0.58 + 2pq$
$2pq = 0.42$

Multiply by 100 to get the percent of heterozygotes to get 42%.

71. Crossing over, which increases genetic diversity occurs during which stage(s)?

    A. telophase II in meiosis
    B. metaphase in mitosis
    C. interphase in both mitosis and meiosis
    D. prophase I in meiosis

D. During prophase I of meiosis, the replicated chromosomes condense and pair with homologues in a process called synapsis. Crossing over, the exchange of genetic material between homologues to further increase diversity, occurs during prophase I.

72. Cancer cells divide extensively and invade other tissues. This continuous cell division is due to

    A. density dependent inhibition
    B. density independent inhibition
    C. chromosome replication
    D. Growth factors

B. Density dependent inhibition is when the cells crowd one another and consume all the nutrients; therefore halting cell division. Cancer cells, however, are density independent; meaning they can divide continuously as long as nutrients are present.

73. Which process(es) results in a haploid chromosome number?

    A. both meiosis and mitosis
    B. mitosis
    C. meiosis
    D. replication and division

C. In meiosis, there are two consecutive cell divisions resulting in the reduction of the chromosome number by half (diploid to haploid).

74. Segments of DNA can be transferred from the DNA of one organism to another through the use of which of the following?

    A. bacterial plasmids
    B. viruses
    C. chromosomes from frogs
    D. plant DNA

A. Plasmids can transfer themselves (and therefore their genetic information) by a process called conjugation. This requires cell-cell contact.

75. Which of the following is not true regarding restriction enzymes?

    A. they do not aid in recombination procedures
    B. they are used in genetic engineering
    C. they are named after the bacteria in which they naturally occur
    D. they identify and splice certain base sequences on DNA

A. A restriction enzyme is a bacterial enzyme that cuts foreign DNA at specific locations. The splicing of restriction fragments into a plasmid results in a recombinant plasmid.

76. A virus that can remain dormant until a certain environmental condition causes its rapid increase is said to be

    A. lytic
    B. benign
    C. saprophytic
    D. lysogenic

D. Lysogenic viruses remain dormant until something initiates it to break out of the host cell.

77. Which is not considered to be a morphological type of bacteria?

    A. obligate
    B. coccus
    C. spirillum
    D. bacillus

A. Morphology is the shape of an organism. Obligate is term used when describing dependence on something. Coccus is a round bacterium, spirillum is a spiral shaped bacterium, and bacillus is a rod shaped bacterium.

78. Antibiotics are effective in fighting bacterial infections due to their ability to

    A. interfere with DNA replication in the bacteria
    B. prevent the formation of new cell walls in the bacteria
    C. disrupt the ribosome of the bacteria
    D. All of the above.

D. Antibiotics can destroy the bacterial cell wall, interfere with bacterial DNA replication, and disrupt the bacterial ribosome without affecting the host cells.

79. Bacteria commonly reproduce by a process called binary fission. Which of the following best defines this process?

A. viral vectors carry DNA to new bacteria
B. DNA from one bacterium enters another
C. DNA doubles and the bacterial cell divides
D. DNA from dead cells is absorbed into bacteria

C. Binary fission is the asexual process in which the bacteria divide in half after the DNA doubles. This results in an exact clone of the parent cell.

80. All of the following are examples of a member of Kingdom Fungi except

A. mold
B. algae
C. mildew
D. mushrooms

B. Mold, mildew, and mushrooms are all fungi. Brown algae and golden algae are members of the kingdom protista and green algae are members of the plant kingdom.

81. Protists are classified into major groups according to

A. their method of obtaining nutrition
B. reproduction
C. metabolism
D. their form and function

D. The chaotic status of names and concepts of the higher classification of the protists reflects their great diversity in form, function, and life styles. The protists are often grouped as algae (plant-like), protozoa (animal-like), or fungus-like based on the similarity of their lifestyle and characteristics to these more derived groups.

82. In comparison to protist cells, moneran cells

    I.   are usually smaller
    II. evolved later
    III. are more complex
    IV. contain more organelles

    A. I
    B. I and II
    C. II and III
    D. I and IV

A.   Moneran cells are almost always smaller than protists. Moneran cells are prokaryotic; therefore they are less complex and have no organelles. Prokaryotes were the first cells on Earth and therefore evolved before than the eukaryotic protists.

83. Spores characterize the reproduction mode for which of the following group of plants?

    A. algae
    B. flowering plants
    C. conifers
    D. ferns

D. Ferns are non-seeded vascular plants. All plants in this group have spores and require water for reproduction. Algae, flowering plants, and conifers are not in this group of plants.

84. Water movement to the top of a twenty foot tree is most likely due to which principle?

    A. osmostic pressure
    B. xylem pressure
    C. capillarity
    D. transpiration

D. Xylem is the tissue that transports water upward. Transpiration is the force that pulls the water upwards. Transpiration is the evaporation of water from leaves.

85.What are the stages of development from the egg to the plant?

    A. morphogenesis, growth, and
       cellular differentiation
    B. cell differentiation, growth, and
       morphogenesis
    C. growth, morphogenesis, and
       cellular differentiation
    D. growth, cellular differentiation,
       and morphogensis

C. The development of the egg to form a plant occurs in three stages: growth; morphogenesis, the development of form; and cellular differentiation, the acquisition of a cell's specific structure and function.

86.In angiosperms, the food for the developing plant is found in which of the following structures?

    A. ovule
    B. endosperm
    C. male gametophyte
    D. cotyledon

B. The endosperm is a product of double fertilization. It is the food supply for the developing plant.

87. The process in which pollen grains are released from the anthers is called

    A. pollination
    B. fertilization
    C. blooming
    D. dispersal

A. Pollen grains are released from the anthers during pollination and carried by animals and the wind to land on the carpels.

88. Which of the following is not a characteristic of a monocot?

    A. parallel veins in leaves
    B. petals of flowers occur in multiples of 4 or 5
    C. one seed leaf
    D. vascular tissue scattered throughout the stem

B. Monocots have one cotelydon, parallel veins in their leaves, and their flower petals are in multiples of threes. Dicots have flower petals in multiples of fours and fives.

89. What controls gas exchange on the bottom of a plant leaf?

    A. stomata
    B. epidermis
    C. collenchyma and schlerenchyma
    D. palisade mesophyll

A. Stomata provide openings on the underside of leaves for oxygen to move in or out of the plant and for carbon dioxide to move in.

90. How are angiosperms different from other groups of plants?

    A. presence of flowers and fruits
    B. production of spores for reproduction
    C. true roots and stems
    D. seed production

A. Angiosperms do not have spores for reproduction. They do have true roots and stems as do all vascular plants. They do have seed production as do the gymnosperms. The presence of flowers and fruits is the difference between angiosperms and other plants.

91. Generations of plants alternate between

    A. angiosperms and bryophytes
    B. flowering and nonflowering stages
    C. seed bearing and spore bearing plants
    D. haploid and diploid stages

D. Reproduction of plants is accomplished through alteration of generations. Simply stated, a haploid stage in the plant's life history alternates with a diploid stage.

92. Double fertilization refers to which choice of the following?

  A. two sperm fertilizing one egg
  B. fertilization of a plant by gametes from two separate plants
  C. two sperm enter the plant embryo sac; one sperm fertilizes the egg, the other forms the endosperm
  D. the production of non-identical twins through fertilization of two separate eggs

C. In angiosperms, double fertilization is when an ovum is fertilized by two sperm. One sperm produces the new plant and the other forms the food supply for the developing plant (endosperm).

93. Characteristics of coelomates include:

  I.   no true digestive system
  II. two germ layers
  III. true fluid filled cavity
  IV. three germ layers

  A. I
  B. II and IV
  C. IV
  D. III and IV

D. Coelomates are triplobastic animals (3 germ layers). They have a true fluid filled body cavity called a coelom.

94. Which phylum accounts for 85% of all animal species?

  A. Nematoda
  B. Chordata
  C. Arthropoda
  D. Cnidaria

C. The arthropoda phylum consists of insects, crustaceans, and spiders. They are the largest group in the animal kingdom.

95. Which is the correct statement regarding the human nervous system and the human endocrine system?

    A. the nervous system maintains homeostasis whereas the endocrine system does not
    B. endocrine glands produce neurotransmitters whereas nerves produce hormones
    C. nerve signals travel on neurons whereas hormones travel through the blood
    D. he nervous system involves chemical transmission whereas the endocrine system does not

C. In the human nervous system, neurons carry nerve signals to and from the cell body. Endocrine glands produce hormones that are carried through the body in the bloodstream.

96. A muscular adaptation to move food through the digestive system is called

    A. peristalsis
    B. passive transport
    C. voluntary action
    D. bulk transport

A. Peristalsis is a process of wave-like contractions. This process allows food to be carried down the pharynx and though the digestive tract.

97. The role of neurotransmitters in nerve action is

    A. turn off sodium pump
    B. turn off calcium pump
    C. send impulse to neuron
    D. send impulse to the body

A. The neurotransmitters turn off the sodium pump which results in depolarization of the membrane.

98. Fats are broken down by which substance?

  A. bile produced in the gall bladder
  B. lipase produced in the gall bladder
  C. glucagons produced in the liver
  D. bile produced in the liver

D. The liver produces bile which breaks down and emulsifies fatty acids.

99. Fertilization in humans usually occurs in the

  A. uterus
  B. ovary
  C. fallopian tubes
  D. vagina

C. Fertilization of the egg by the sperm normally occurs in the fallopian tube. The fertilized egg is then implanted on the uterine lining for development.

100. All of the following are found in the dermis layer of skin except

  A. sweat glands
  B. keratin
  C. hair follicles
  D. blood vessels

B. Keratin is a water proofing protein found in the epidermis.

101. Which is the correct sequence of embryonic development in a frog?

  A. cleavage – blastula – gastrula
  B. cleavage – gastrula – blastula
  C. blastula – cleavage – gastrula
  D. gastrula – blastula – cleavage

A. Animals go through several stages of development after fertilization of the egg cell. The first step is cleavage which continues until the egg becomes a blastula. The blastula is a hollow ball of undifferentiated cells. Gastrulation is the next step. This is the time of tissue differentiation into the separate germ layers: the endoderm, mesoderm, and ectoderm.

102. Food is carried through the digestive tract by a series of wave-like contractions. This process is called

   A. peristalsis
   B. chyme
   C. digestion
   D. absorption

A. Peristalsis is the process of wave-like contractions that moves food through the digestive tract.

103. Movement is possible by the action of muscles pulling on

   A. skin
   B. bones
   C. joints
   D. ligaments

B. The muscular system's function is for movement. Skeletal muscles are attached to bones and are responsible for their movement.

104. All of the following are functions of the skin except

   A. storage
   B. protection
   C. sensation
   D. regulation of temperature

A. Skin is a protective barrier against infection. It contains hair follicles that respond to sensation and it plays a role in thermoregulation.

105. Hormones are essential to the regulation of reproduction. What organ is responsible for the release of hormones for sexual maturity?

   A. pituitary gland
   B. hypothalamus
   C. pancreas
   D. thyroid gland

B. The hypothalamus begins secreting hormones that help mature the reproductive system and development of the secondary sex characteristics.

106. **A bicyclist has a heart rate of 110 beats per minute and a stroke volume of 85 mL per beat. What is the cardiac output?**

    A. 9.35 L/min
    B. 1.29 L/min
    C. 0.772 L/min
    D. 129 L/min

A. The cardiac output is the volume of blood per minute that is pumped into the systemic circuit. This is determined by the heart rate and the stroke volume. Multiply the heart rate by the stroke volume. 110 * 85 = 9350 mL/min. Divide by 1000 to get units of liters. 9350/1000 = 9.35 L/min.

107. **After sea turtles are hatched on the beach, they start the journey to the ocean. This is due to**

    A. innate behavior
    B. territoriality
    C. the tide
    D. learned behavior

A. Innate behavior are inborn or instinctual. The baby sea turtles did not learn from their mother. They immediately knew to head towards the ocean once they hatched.

108. **A school age boy had the chicken pox as a baby. He will most likely not get this disease again because of**

    A. passive immunity
    B. vaccination
    C. antibiotics
    D. active immunity

D. Active immunity develops after recovery from an infectious disease, such as the chicken pox, or after vaccination. Passive immunity may be passed from one individual to another (from mother to nursing child).

109. High humidity and temperature stability are present in which of the following biomes?

    A. taiga
    B. deciduous forest
    C. desert
    D. tropical rain forest

D. A tropical rain forest is located near the equator. Its temperature is at a constant 25 degrees C and the humidity is high due to the rainfall that exceeds 200 cm per year.

110. The biological species concept applies to

    A. asexual organisms
    B. extinct organisms
    C. sexual organisms
    D. fossil organisms

C. The biological species concept states that a species is a reproductive community of populations that occupy a specific niche in nature. It focuses on reproductive isolation of populations as the primary criterion for recognition of species status. The biological species concept does not apply to organisms that are completely asexual in their reproduction, fossil organisms, or distinctive populations that hybridize.

111. Which term is not associated with the water cycle?

    A. precipitation
    B. transpiration
    C. fixation
    D. evaporation

C. Water is recycled through the processes of evaporation and precipitation. Transpiration is the evaporation of water from leaves. Fixation is not associated with the water cycle.

112. All of the following are density independent factors that affect a population except

A. temperature
B. rainfall
C. predation
D. soil nutrients

C. As a population increases, the competition for resources is intense and the growth rate declines. This is a density-dependent factor. An example of this would be predation. Density-independent factors affect the population regardless of its size. Examples of density-independent factors are rainfall, temperature, and soil nutrients.

113. In the growth of a population, the increase is exponential until carrying capacity is reached. This is represented by a (n)

A. S curve
B. J curve
C. M curve
D. L curve

A. An exponentially growing population starts off with little change and then rapidly increases. The graphic representation of this growth curve has the appearance of a "J". However, as the carrying capacity of the exponentially growing population is reached, the growth rate begins to slow down and level off. The graphic representation of this growth curve has the appearance of an "S".

114. Primary succession occurs after

A. nutrient enrichment
B. a forest fire
C. bare rock is exposed after a water table recedes
D. a housing development is built

C. Primary succession occurs where life never existed before, such as flooded areas or a new volcanic island. It is only after the water recedes that the rock is able to support new life.

115. Crabgrass – grasshopper – frog – snake – eagle If DDT were present in an ecosystem, which organism would have the highest concentration in its system?

A. grasshopper
B. eagle
C. frog
D. crabgrass

B. Chemicals and pesticides accumulate along the food chain. Tertiary consumers have more accumulated toxins than animals at the bottom of the food chain.

116. Which trophic level has the highest ecological efficiency?

A. decomposers
B. producers
C. tertiary consumers
D. secondary consumers

B. The amount of energy that is transferred between trophic levels is called the ecological efficiency. The visual of this is represented in a pyramid of productivity. The producers have the greatest amount of energy and are at the bottom of this pyramid.

117. A clownfish is protected by the sea anemone's tentacles. In turn, the anemone receives uneaten food from the clownfish. This is an example of

A. mutualism
B. parasitism
C. commensalisms
D. competition

A. Neither the clownfish nor the anemone cause harmful effects towards one another and they both benefit from their relationship. Mutualism is when two species that occupy a similar space benefit from their relationship.

118. If the niches of two species overlap, what usually results?

    A. a symbiotic relationship
    B. cooperation
    C. competition
    D. a new species

C. Two species that occupy the same habitat or eat the same food are said to be in competition with each other.

119. Oxygen created in photosynthesis comes from the breakdown of

    A. carbon dioxide
    B. water
    C. glucose
    D. carbon monoxide

B. In photosynthesis, water is split; the hydrogen atoms are pulled to carbon dioxide which is taken in by the plant and ultimately reduced to make glucose. The oxygen from the water is given off as a waste product.

120. Which photosystem makes ATP?

    A. photosystem I
    B. photosystem II
    C. photosystem III
    D. photosystem IV

A. Photosystem I is composed of a pair of chlorophyll *a* molecules It makes ATP whose energy is needed to build glucose.

121. All of the following gasses made up the primitive atmosphere except

    A. ammonia
    B. methane
    C. oxygen
    D. hydrogen

C. In the 1920s, Oparin and Haldane were to first to theorize that the primitive atmosphere was a reducing atmosphere with no oxygen. The gases were rich in hydrogen, methane, water, and ammonia.

122. The Endosymbiotic theory states that

    A. eukaryotes arose from prokaryotes
    B. animals evolved in close relationships with one another
    C. the prokaryotes arose from eukaryotes
    D. life arose from inorganic compounds

A. The Endosymbiotic theory of the origin of eukaryotes states that eukaryotes arose from symbiotic groups of prokaryotic cells. According to this theory, smaller prokaryotes lived within larger prokaryotic cells, eventually evolving into chloroplasts and mitochondria.

123. Which aspect of science does not support evolution?

    A. comparative anatomy
    B. organic chemistry
    C. comparison of DNA among organisms
    D. analogous structures

B. Comparative anatomy is the comparison of characteristics of the anatomies of different species. This includes homologous structures and analogous structures. The comparison of DNA between species is the best known way to place species on the evolution tree. Organic chemistry has nothing to do with evolution.

124. Evolution occurs in

    A. individuals
    B. populations
    C. organ systems
    D. cells

B. Evolution is a change in genotype over time. Gene frequencies shift and change from generation to generation. Populations evolve, not individuals.

125. Which process contributes to the large variety of living things in the world today?

    A. meiosis
    B. asexual reproduction
    C. mitosis
    D. alternation of generations

A. During meiosis prophase I crossing over occurs. This exchange of genetic material between homologues increases diversity.

126. The wing of bird, human arm and whale flipper have the same bone structure. These are called

    A. polymorphic structures
    B. homologous structures
    C. vestigial structures
    D. analogous structures

B. Homologous characteristics have the same genetic basis (leading to similar appearances) but are used for a different function.

127. Which biome is the most prevalent on Earth?

    A. marine
    B. desert
    C. savanna
    D. tundra

A. The marine biome covers 75% of the Earth. This biome is organized by the depth of water.

128. Which of the following is not an abiotic factor?

    A. temperature
    B. rainfall
    C. soil quality
    D. bacteria

D. Abiotic factors are non-living aspects of an ecosystem. Bacteria is an example of a biotic factor—a living thing in an ecosystem.

129. DNA synthesis results in a strand that is synthesized continuously. This is the

    A. lagging strand
    B. leading strand
    C. template strand
    D. complementary strand

B. As DNA synthesis proceeds along the replication fork, one strand is replicated continuously (the leading strand) and the other strand is replicated discontinuously (lagging strand).

130. Using a gram staining technique, it is observed that E. coli stains pink. It is therefore

    A. gram positive
    B. dead
    C. gram negative
    D. gram neutral

C. A Gram positive bacterium absorbs the stain and appears purple under a microscope because of its cell wall made of peptidoglycan. A Gram negative bacterium does not absorb the stain because of its more complex cell wall. These bacteria appear pink under a microscope.

131. A light microscope has an ocular of 10X and an objective of 40X. What is the total magnification?

    A. 400X
    B. 30X
    C. 50X
    D. 4000X

A. To determine the total magnification of a microscope, multiply the ocular lens by the objective lens. Here, the ocular lens is 10X and the objective lens is 40X.

    (10X) X (40X) = 400X total magnification

132. Three plants were grown. The following data was taken. Determine the mean growth.

Plant 1: 10cm Plant 2: 20cm Plant 3: 15cm

A. 5 cm
B. 45 cm
C. 12 cm
D. 15 cm

D. The mean growth is the average of the three growth heights.

$$\frac{10 + 20 + 15}{3} = 15\text{cm average height}$$

133. Electrophoresis separates DNA on the basis of

A. amount of current
B. molecular size
C. positive charge of the molecule
D. solubility of the gel

B. Electrophoresis uses electrical charges of molecules to separate them according to their size.

134. The reading of a meniscus in a graduated cylinder is done at the

A. top of the meniscus
B. middle of the meniscus
C. bottom of the meniscus
D. closest whole number

C. The graduated cylinder is the common instrument used for measuring volume. It is important for the accuracy of the measurement to read the volume level of the liquid at the bottom of the meniscus. The meniscus is the curved surface of the liquid.

135. Two hundred plants were grown. Fifty plants died. What percentage of the plants survived?

A. 40%
B. 25%
C. 75%
D. 50%

C. This is a proportion. If 50 plants died, then 200 – 50 = 150 survived. The number of survivors is the numerator and the total number of plants grown is the denominator.

$$\frac{150}{200} = 0.75 \text{ Multiply by 100 to get percent} = 75\% \text{ survive}$$

136. Which is not a correct statement regarding the use of a light microscope?

A. carry the microscope with two hands
B. store on the low power objective
C. clean all lenses with lens paper
D. Focus first on high power

D. Always begin focusing on low power. This allows for the observation of microorganisms in a larger field of view. Switch to high power once you have a microorganism in view on low power.

137. Spectrophotometry utilizes the principle of

A. light transmission
B. molecular weight
C. solubility of the substance
D. electrical charges

A. Spectrophotometry uses percent of light at different wavelengths absorbed and transmitted by a pigment solution.

138. Chromotography is most often associated with the separation of

    A. nutritional elements
    B. DNA
    C. proteins
    D. plant pigments

D. Chromatography uses the principles of capillarity to separate substances such as plant pigments. Molecules of a larger size will move slower up the paper, whereas smaller molecules will move more quickly producing lines of pigment.

139. A genetic engineering advancement in the medical field is

    A. gene therapy
    B. pesticides
    C. degradation of harmful chemicals
    D. antibiotics

A. Gene therapy is the introduction of a normal allele to the somatic cells to replace a defective allele. The medical field has had success in treating patients with a single enzyme deficiency disease. Gene therapy has allowed doctors and scientists to introduce a normal allele that would provide the missing enzyme.

140. Which scientists are credited with the discovery of the structure of DNA?

    A. Hershey & Chase
    B. Sutton & Morgan
    C. Watson & Crick
    D. Miller & Fox

C. In the 1950s, James Watson and Francis Crick discovered the structure of a DNA molecule as that of a double helix.

141. Negatively charged particles that circle the nucleus of an atom are called

    A. neutrons
    B. neutrinos
    C. electrons
    D. protons

C. Neutrons and protons make up the core of an atom. Neutrons have no charge and protons are positively charged. Electrons are the negatively charged particles around the nucleus.

142. The shape of a cell depends on its

    A. function
    B. structure
    C. age
    D. size

A. In most living organisms, its structure is based on its function.

143. The most ATP is generated through

    A. fermentation
    B. glycolysis
    C. chemiosmosis
    D. Krebs cycle

C. The electron transport chain uses electrons to pump hydrogen ions across the mitochondrial membrane. This ion gradient is used to form ATP in a process called chemiosmosis. ATP is generated by the movement of hydrogen ions off NADH and $FADH_2$. This yields 34 ATP molecules.

144. In DNA, adenine bonds with _____, while cytosine bonds with _____.

    A. thymine/guanine
    B. adenine/cytosine
    C. cytosine/adenine
    D. guanine/thymine

A. In DNA, adenine pairs with thymine and cytosine pairs with guanine because of their nitrogenous base structures.

145. The individual parts of cells are best studied using a (n)

A. ultracentrifuge
B. phase-contrast microscope
C. CAT scan
D. electron microscope

D. The scanning electron microscope uses a beam of electrons to pass through the specimen. The resolution is about 1000 times greater than that of a light microscope. This allows the scientist to view extremely small objects, such as the individual parts of a cell.

146. Thermoacidophiles are

A. prokaryotes
B. eukaryotes
C. protists
D. archaea

D. Thermoacidophiles, methanogens, and halobacteria are members of the archaea group. They are as diverse from prokaryotes as prokaryotes are to eukaryotes.

147. Which of the following is not a type of fiber that makes up the cytoskeleton?

A. vacuoles
B. microfilaments
C. microtubules
D. intermediate filaments

A. Vacuoles are mostly found in plants and hold stored food and pigments. The other three choices are fibers that make up the cytoskeleton found in both plant and animal cells.

148. Viruses are made of

A. a protein coat surrounding a nucleic acid
B. DNA, RNA and a cell wall
C. a nucleic acid surrounding a protein coat
D. protein surrounded by DNA

A. Viruses are composed of a protein coat and a nucleic acid; either RNA or DNA.

149. Reproductive isolation results in

A. extinction
B. migration
C. follilization
D. speciation

D. Reproductive isolation is caused by any factor that impedes two species from producing viable, fertile hybrids. Reproductive isolation of populations is the primary criterion for recognition of species status.

150. This protein structure consists of the coils and folds of polypeptide chains. Which is it?

A. secondary structure
B. quaternary structure
C. tertiary structure
D. primary structure

A. Primary structure is the protein's unique sequence of amino acids. Secondary structure is the coils and folds of polypeptide chains. The coils and folds are the result of hydrogen bonds along the polypeptide backbone. Tertiary structure is formed by bonding between the side chains of the amino acids. Quaternary structure is the overall structure of the protein from the aggregation of two or more polypeptide chains.

XAMonline, INC. 21 Orient Ave. Melrose, MA 02176

Toll Free number 800-509-4128

TO ORDER Fax 781-662-9268 OR www.XAMonline.com

MICHIGAN TEST FOR TEACHER EXAMINATION - MTTC - 2007

PO#   Store/School:

Address 1:

Address 2 (Ship to other):

City, State Zip

Credit card number_____-_____-_____-_____   expiration_____

EMAIL _____

PHONE   **FAX**

13# ISBN 2007	TITLE	Qty	Retail	Total
978-1-58197-968-8	MTTC Basic Skills 96			
978-1-58197-954-1	MTTC Biology 17			
978-1-58197-955-8	MTTC Chemistry 18			
978-1-58197-957-2	MTTC Earth-Space Science 20			
978-1-58197-966-4	MTTC Elementary Education 83			
978-1-58197-967-1	MTTC Elementary Education 83 Sample Questions			
978-1-58197-950-3	MTTC English 02			
978-1-58197-961-9	MTTC Family and Consumer Sciences 40			
978-1-58197-959-6	MTTC French Sample Test 23			
978-1-58197-965-7	MTTC Guidance Counselor 51			
978-1-58197-964-0	MTTC Humanities& Fine Arts 53, 54			
978-1-58197-972-5	MTTC Integrated Science (Secondary) 94			
978-1-58197-973-2	MTTC Emotionally Impaired 59			
978-1-58197-953-4	MTTC Learning Disabled 63			
978-1-58197-963-3	MTTC Library Media 48			
978-1-58197-958-9	MTTC Mathematics (Secondary) 22			
978-1-58197-962-6	MTTC Physical Education 44			
978-1-58197-956-5	MTTC Physics Sample Test 19			
978-1-58197-952-7	MTTC Political Science 10			
978-1-58197-951-0	MTTC Reading 05			
978-1-58197-960-2	MTTC Spanish 28			
978-158197-970-1	MTTC Social Studies 84			

	SUBTOTAL	
FOR PRODUCT PRICES GO TO WWW.XAMONLINE.COM	Ship	$8.25
	TOTAL	